Demystifying Decision-Making

Demystifying Decision-Making

A Practical Guide

Aimee Joseph

CROSSWAY®

WHEATON, ILLINOIS

Trade paperback ISBN: 978-1-4335-7541-9
ePub ISBN: 978-1-4335-7544-0
PDF ISBN: 978-1-4335-7542-6
Mobipocket ISBN: 978-1-4335-7543-3

Library of Congress Cataloging-in-Publication Data

Names: Joseph, Aimee, 1983- author.
Title: Demystifying decision-making : a practical guide / Aimee Joseph.
Description: Wheaton, Illinois : Crossway, 2022. | Series: The gospel coalition | Includes bibliographical references and index.
Identifiers: LCCN 2021012806 (print) | LCCN 2021012807 (ebook) | ISBN 9781433575419 (trade paperback) | ISBN 9781433575426 (pdf) | ISBN 9781433575433 (mobipocket) | ISBN 9781433575440 (epub)
Subjects: LCSH: Decision making—Religious aspects—Christianity.
Classification: LCC BV4509.5 .J678 2022 (print) | LCC BV4509.5 (ebook) | DDC 248.4—dc23
LC record available at https://lccn.loc.gov/2021012806
LC ebook record available at https://lccn.loc.gov/2021012807

Crossway is a publishing ministry of Good News Publishers.

BP		31	30	29	28	27	26	25	24	23	22
15	14	13	12	11	10	9	8	7	6	5	4	3	2	1

To G'Joe, Tyus, Eli, and Phin

All the way may the Savior lead us.

Contents

Introduction

Ubiquitous Decisions

SOMETIMES THINGS BECOME so much a part of the fabric of our lives that we don't even recognize them. Decisions are chief among them. They are so ubiquitous that we tend to drown out their prevalence and significance.

In a self-initiated experiment, I decided to keep a running tally of the number of decisions I made throughout an average day. Before my feet even hit the ground, I had counted four: *Do I sleep five more minutes? Do I shower now or after my morning walk? When should I take the dog for a walk? What shall I wear today?*

Next, I stared down a significant breakfast decision. I landed on cereal but then had to decide which cereal, which bowl, and which milk. As soon as those decisions were settled, I faced coffee decisions: *travel mug or regular mug? Sugar or Splenda?*

At this point, I had been awake only three minutes. *Where will I sit to spend time with God? Should I journal or read the Bible? Assuming I decide to start with reading the Bible, where shall I read this morning? How many verses?* We are only ten minutes into the day. Suffice it to say that after an hour I promptly quit the exercise, utterly overwhelmed by the sheer number of decisions that make up an ordinary day.

If you are not convinced by my experiment, I'd like to invite you into a short trip to the local grocery store. We aren't shopping for a Thanksgiving meal. We only need the ingredients for an apple pie. Sounds simple enough, right? Before we even get to the store, we must decide which parking spot to choose based on which entrance we will walk through. Then we must choose whether to get the wonky-wheeled shopping cart or risk nearly breaking our wrists carrying a basket. Friends, we are not yet fully in the store. We approach the produce section with a simple need: apples. What used to be a semi-simple choice between green or red has become a complex decision these days. *Pink Lady, Gala, Red Delicious, or Fuji? Organic or regular?* Next comes flour. *Almond flour? Whole wheat flour? Enriched flour? Store brand or name brand?* Regarding eggs, we have an entire endcap from which to choose. *Regular eggs, organic eggs, free-range eggs, and local eggs (*and every possible combination of these categories). I won't belabor the point. You live in the same world I do. We experience the same decision-making fatigue. Thus far we are only making an apple pie. We have not even broached the subject of the weightier decisions of life.

The Dizziness of Decisions

Søren Kierkegaard, the Danish theologian and philosopher, once said, "Anxiety is the dizziness of freedom." If grocery store decisions make us dizzy, the more significant decisions of our lives cause deeper and more disorienting anxiety. One of the unanticipated weights of living in an age of unprecedented freedom is the anxiety that comes as its counterpart.

In the past (and in other cultures in the present), freedom was much more limited. Most children were not able to choose a calling or direction. They would learn the family trade that had been passed down from generation to generation. Likewise, it was assumed that they would remain in the hometown that the family had lived in for generations.

My parents-in-law were born in neighboring villages in Kerala, India. My amma had two career choices: nurse or teacher. When my appa was young, he knew he would study engineering as his father and uncles had. Amma and Appa did not even play a primary role in choosing to marry one another; their parents arranged their marriage. The second time they met, they were walking down the aisle and into their future. After having twins (one of whom is now my handsome husband), they emigrated to the United States in search of a better future and more opportunities for their children.

Flash-forward twenty years. My husband and I sit around Amma and Appa's kitchen table in Austin, Texas, with our three children. My middle son has been tasked with preparing a heritage report for his class. We huddle around the table as a captive audience as my son interviews my in-laws. When asked about their childhood in India, both Amma and Appa smile as they reminisce. "It was so carefree; we played all the time. We did not have the stress and the worry. We were just children."

My children have far more choices than Amma and Appa had at their age. They can choose from five different club soccer teams. They select multiple elective courses even at their elementary school. Shows, books, and role models regularly remind them to be whoever and whatever they want to be. For now, these promises of choice and freedom sound alluring. However, in less than ten years my oldest son will likely be graduating from college. Suddenly the freedom to be and do whatever he wants will transform into the intense, crushing anxiety that is the dizziness of freedom. Professors and well-intentioned friends will be asking him a litany of questions. *What are you going to do when you graduate? To which graduate schools have you applied? Where will you live?*

In a culture marked by freedom yet marred by anxiety, the decision-making process confuses us. Some decisions paralyze us, while other decisions pass by seemingly unnoticed.

The Shaping Power of Decisions

In his short but powerful book *The Death of Ivan Ilyich*, Leo Tolstoy brings us to the deathbed of an average Russian man. Ivan, like most of us, did not take the time to think about his daily decisions. Life was so full, so promising, so busy with its demands and desires, that Ivan simply went along for the ride. The currents of culture and the tyranny of the moment directed his life. He attended the popular parties, married into the right class, and worked hard as a lawyer to purchase the right fabric for the right drapes to meet the current fashions. His life came to a screeching halt with the diagnosis of a terminal illness.

Tolstoy invites us into the moment in which Ivan, an unreflective man, must face the cumulative effect of his life decisions. He lived his life as "a capable, cheerful, good-natured, and sociable man." He did whatever his station and culture dictated to be fashionable. When institutions and fashions changed, he adjusted accordingly. He climbed the social and professional ladders. He married well, even if not for love. Tolstoy leads the reader through Ivan's decisions in the same matter-of-fact way that Ivan made them. Ivan and his wife bore children. They hit a few rough patches financially and eventually rebounded. After moving into a new home, Tolstoy writes the following about Ivan and his family:

> And so, they began to live in their new quarters which, as always happens when people get settled, was just one room too small, and on their new income, which, as is always the case, was just a bit less—about five hundred rubles—than they needed. But it was all very nice.[1]

In a way that seems almost laughable to the reader, Tolstoy describes the ordinariness of Ivan's life. A series of decisions stacking up. Tolstoy summarizes a lifetime of decisions in a few sentences, saying, "So they lived. Everything went along without change and everything was fine."[2]

Until it wasn't.

After being diagnosed with a life-threatening illness, Ivan's perspective began to change. His terminal illness cast decisions he thought were pleasant inevitabilities in a different light. Tolstoy captures Ivan's significant moment of realization:

> And in his imagination, he called to mind the best moments of his pleasant life. Yet, strangely enough, all the best moments of his pleasant life now seemed entirely different than they had in the past. . . . "Perhaps I did not live as I should have," it

suddenly occurred to him. "But how could that be when I did everything one is supposed to?"[3]

Our culture constantly reminds us to take each moment as it comes and to live for today. Ivan Illyich did those things. He made decisions based on the culture around him and the desires within him; however, at the end of his life, his decisions proved disappointing. How can we avoid finding ourselves in Ivan's shoes? To what cumulative end are our daily decisions directing us?

Divine Direction in Decisions

If you are reading this book, I imagine I don't have to convince you of the dizziness of decisions or their power to shape our lives. You are likely living in the crosshairs of critical decisions. Perhaps you are wondering which path to take, which church to choose, or which spouse to marry. No matter what decision you are deliberating, the incredibly good news is that the Scriptures offer guidance for believers making decisions.

God graciously stamped humanity in his image, giving us the ability to make decisions (Gen. 1:27). By his very nature, God is self-revelatory, meaning he wants to be known, seen, worshiped, and followed. God is not a divine clockmaker who created the universe and then stepped away to let it run. Rather, he has intimately involved himself in his creation from the beginning.

Even after God's people alienated themselves from him through their sin, God moved toward them and directed them (Gen. 3:8–10). He created for himself a people whom he would lead (Gen. 12:1–9). He sent prophets to speak to them, priests to atone for them, and kings to lead them. His engagement with his decision-making people came to a culmination in the incarnation of Christ (John 1:6–14). Christ made the invisible God visible in a tangible way (Heb. 1:3). Christ walked this earth and experienced the daily decisions of life. Though he was tempted in every way as we are (Heb. 4:15), he made every decision considering the favor of his father. He chose to follow God even when that choice meant death on a cross (Phil. 2:8).

Through the life, death, and resurrection of Christ, believers are invited into the freedom of making decisions as children of God. Rather than following the whims of their heart, believers are invited to place the desires of their hearts alongside the word of God as a ruler. God's word, God's Spirit, and God's people are intended to help instruct us in the series of decisions that constitutes life.

The Path before Us

Judging from the number of books and articles promising five steps to better decisions or the secret to discovering calling, people hunger for practical wisdom and guidance. We want to know which way to go, which house to buy, or which college to attend. We are eager to be given the answer; however, before we can jump into practical decision-making, it is necessary that we lay a theological foundation. While God's word can practically guide us, God intends his word to do something far more profound.

In *Mere Christianity*, C. S. Lewis paints a powerful word picture:

Imagine yourself as a living house. God comes in to rebuild that house. At first, perhaps, you can understand what He is doing. He is getting the drains right and stopping the leaks in the roof and so on; you knew that those jobs needed doing and so you are not surprised. But presently He starts knocking the house about in a way that hurts abominably and does not seem to make any sense. What on earth is He up to? The explanation is that He is building quite a different house from the one you thought of—throwing out a new wing here, putting on an extra floor there, running up towers, making courtyards. You thought you were being made into a decent little cottage: but He is building a palace. He intends to come and live in it Himself.[4]

People are drawn to books that address their problem, their proverbial leaky faucet. While I do hope that this book will address that leaky faucet of yours, I also expect that it will knock down a few walls and change your design-making blueprint. Before we can get to practical decision-making, we should address existing frameworks, potentially razing them that we might raise up a biblically and theologically informed framework. Questions for further discussion are included in the back of the book. Whether you are working through this book alone, with a mentor, or with a group of trusted friends, these questions are intended to help you reflect upon, synthesize, and apply the principles we will learn.

In chapters 1 and 2 we will explore God's design in creating human beings as decision makers. We will learn the great responsibility and privilege entrusted to us as we sift through what choices and consequences mean in light of the cross. We will also wrestle through the apparent contradictions between God's sovereignty and man's responsibility. Most significantly, we will stand at the foot of the cross to be reminded that God views us through the faithful decisions of Christ even amid our failures and shortcomings (2 Cor. 5:21).

In chapters 3 and 4 we will unpack various concepts of God's will and discover the distinction between his hidden will and his revealed will. Once we get our biblical bearings, we will address common approaches to making decisions and the dashboards we consult in making decisions. In chapters 5 and 6 we will familiarize ourselves with tools that God provides as we prepare for and make decisions. Finally, in chapter 7, we will address the regret, fear, and pride that often await us after decisions have been made. The same God who offers us wisdom in making decisions also secures peace for us on the other side of decision-making.

I wish we could sit down over coffee to discuss the dilemma or decision you face. It would be an honor and a privilege to hear your story and learn about the various decisions that may have led you to this book. Alas, by its limited nature, a book on decision-making in general may fail to address "the holy particularity of the soul in need."[5] However, I have been expectantly praying that God would use this little book as a pointer to Christ, the one who meets the needs of his creation with his abundant wisdom and love. I am asking that the same Lord who brings order out of chaos might begin to part the clouds that confuse the decision-making process. I have confidence that the clarity of his word and the absolute nature of his character will demystify the process and lead you into the freedom and privilege of making decisions as his image bearers on this earth.

1

The Drama of Decisions

DECISION-MAKING IS OFTEN DRAMATIC, even for undramatic people. Think about the last show you binge-watched or the latest novel you stayed up late to finish. Chances are you were gripped by the drama of a decision faced by one of the characters. The Mandalorian decides between bounty hunting and rescuing the Child, Josephine March waffles between love and independence, and Katniss Everdeen vacillates between Peeta or Gale. In all ages and places, people (real and imagined) choose what they believe is best based on a myriad of factors. In order to understand the way we make decisions today, let's take a moment to survey decision-making throughout human history.

Decision-Making throughout History

From the beginning of recorded history, people have wrestled with the decisions of their lives. For centuries, people based their decision-making on a desire to discern the will of the gods. Decision-making began with the presupposition that the gods were interested in what people did and demanded to be pleased, or at least appeased, by human choices. Even a cursory reading of ancient Greek and Roman mythology reveals the deep human desire to discern what might please the fickle gods. Humans cowered in fear or relied on cunning and trickery to stay away from the wrath of their pantheon of gods and goddesses, each of whom operated out of their own whims. Their gods were moving targets, which left them uneasy when making decisions. Imagine never knowing whether your choice of a spouse would result in blessing or a lethal firebolt from Mount Olympus! As a result, humans resorted to divination: strange and diverse methods of attempting to discern the will of their gods.

Divination

Many pagan cultures practiced *hepatoscopy*, which was the study of the liver. To our modern minds, the liver sounds like a strange place to start; however, they believed the liver, the heaviest organ, housed memory and intelligence. Thus it made logical sense to them that if the gods wanted to reveal themselves to them, they would do so through the liver.

Another pagan ritual to discern the will of the gods was called "rhabdomancy." In this method people used arrows to help determine what the gods willed. Supposedly, the flight of the arrow and its landing place provided direction in decisions. Other methods for divination included the use of household idols called "teraphim" as well as palm reading and astrology.[1]

Twenty-First-Century Divination

While those methods sound rudimentary and strange to our ears, it's helpful to consider some of our own postmodern attempts to understand what God wants for our decisions. Some people still dabble in astrology, horoscopes, and fortune-telling when considering major life decisions today. In fact, upon moving to Southern California from the Southeast, I was shocked at how many of my new neighbors mentioned their astrological symbols as significant factors in their decisions. In conversations, a friend would casually say, "I am a Pisces, so I love the beach," or, "My horoscope mentioned that good things were coming my way this month." I did my best to stifle my shock, as I had wrongly thought palm readers and tarot cards were mostly artifacts or the stuff of movies. The number of New Age shops advertising these services within a 10-mile radius of my home tells me otherwise.

Astrology and other New Age aids in decision-making are somewhat right in lifting hungry, searching eyes up to the skies; however, they stop short by looking at the canvas of creation rather than looking further back to the knowable Creator. The further our postmodern culture pushes back from its Judeo-Christian roots, the more people grasp for ancient avenues for divine help and direction. As Solomon insightfully wrote in Ecclesiastes 3:11, God "has put eternity into man's heart." Try as we might to exclude God from the picture, he keeps finding his way back into our hearts because they were made for eternity.

Even within the Christian faith, many believers fall back upon ancient methods for discerning God's will, begging for signs of God's direction in big decisions. Believers do this partly because they do not understand the nature of God and his means of revealing his will.

Reason Alone

Most people believe that God has nothing to do with our lives and choices at all. As those born after the age of reason, many twenty-first-century minds approach decision-making as if it were an entirely rational process. If we were to assign the rational approach a representative symbol, it would likely be a list of pros and cons. While a well-thought-out list of pros and cons provides helpful perspective in making decisions, reason alone addresses only one aspect of humanity. It raises the mind over and against the will and the body, pressing significant God-given parts of our lives out of the process.

We have been deeply marked by Enlightenment ideals. Our overestimation of the human capacity to reason pushes God to the periphery. Some of us seem to have forgotten that decision-making began from a deep desire to understand God's will.

Follow Your Heart

Chances are that most of your neighbors are neither mystics nor rationalists. Chances are that most of them ascribe to some version of the popular modern mantra, "Follow your heart." According to this prevalent perspective, whatever feels right, looks good, or seems best *is* best. As long as no one gets hurt, your choices are entirely up to you and what you want. This line of thinking sounds good to us initially. In fact, I remember a friend in high school making me a little sign with the pithy quote, "In matters of the head, think with the head; in matters of the heart, think with the heart." I liked it so much that I hung it on my wall. It would be a few years before I realized that such reasoning, beautiful though it sounded, was both unhelpful and unbiblical.

As we will discuss in chapter 4, God has knit us together body, mind, and soul. This means that our emotions and desires matter in the decision-making process; however, the fall of mankind into sin affects both our minds and our emotions. In other words, the fall affects our affections (a fancy, old-fashioned word for feelings). Our feelings, inclinations, and preferences must be washed in the word and sanctified. As early as Saint Augustine and Jonathan Edwards, Christian theologians have fought to keep religious affections a significant part of the Christian life.[2] While affections have a role to play in making decisions, they are not to have the final word; Christ alone gets that distinction.

Each of these approaches gets something right and something wrong. Contemporary mystics rightly claim that we must acknowledge something outside ourselves when making choices, but they don't understand the nature of the true God. Contemporary rationalists rightly use faculties of reason and logic to make choices, but they don't acknowledge the God who is sovereign over the minds of all people. Contemporary heart followers rightly know that what we want has a legitimate place in our goals, but they don't recognize the deceitfulness of the sinful heart or the lordship of God over our desires.

To properly understand the full picture of our framework for decision-making, the best place to begin is with the Bible.

Why Am I Here?

While many of us don't realize it, our worldview influences the way we approach decisions. A worldview provides the framework through which we see, understand, and process all of life. Every worldview answers four main questions regarding human life: "Why am I here?" "What went wrong with the world?" "What is the solution?" and "Where is history heading?" While these questions may sound ethereal, their answers have incredibly real results in our day-to-day lives.

Even those who would not consider themselves religious adhere to some form of a worldview. Atheists have a certain view of the world, and this view cannot be separated from the way they approach decisions. For example, someone who does not believe in a supernatural being likely lives by the mantra, "Let us eat, drink, and be merry, for tomorrow we die." If our lives are confined to the actual years we live on the earth, then such a short-term view will inform the daily habits of those who adhere to this view.

Thankfully, God has not left us to our own devices to answer these worldview questions. Unlike the pagan gods that were mere inventions of the people who believed in them, God has given us his inspired, inerrant, and infallible word. The first two chapters of Genesis answer our questions regarding the origin and purpose of human life.

In Genesis 1:26, we find the members of the Trinity talking among themselves about their purposes in creating humanity, saying, "Let us make man in our image, after our likeness." Humanity was not created out of boredom or some other lack in our God, but rather out of the fullness of the Trinity. We were created in the image of a relational and personal God who is self-revelatory. We were created out of relationship and for relationship. Thus the decisions we make about where to work, whom to marry, how to spend our money and time, and the myriad of other questions we rightly ask should be made within the backdrop of our relationship to God and his purposes for humanity at large.

When God created us and uniquely stamped us with his image, he set us apart from the rest of creation. As the psalmist poetically muses, "When I look at your heavens, the work of your fingers, the moon and the stars, which you have set in place, what is man that you are mindful of him, and the son of man that you care for him?" (Ps. 8:3–4).

As his image bearers, we have souls that have been breathed to life by the very breath of God (Gen. 2:7). We have the capacity to reason, create, and communicate. In creating us, God granted us the ability to choose freely. In God's place we might have chosen to create automatons programmed always and only to do our will; however, God wanted a volitional relationship with us. As such, he gave Adam and Eve real boundaries and real choices with real consequences. Having provided them with everything they could possibly need and beyond, he commanded Adam, who was to inform Eve, "You may surely eat of every tree of the garden, but of the tree of the knowledge of good and evil you shall not eat, for in the day that you eat of it you shall surely die" (Gen. 2:16–17).

Ample trees grew for their enjoyment. It was the orchard of all orchards. They had everything they needed, yet in their free will, they chose to disobey God by eating from the one tree forbidden them. Lured by the lies of the great enemy of God, a former angel who wanted more power than he was given, they began to doubt the character and goodness of their Creator God. Believing the lie that he was withholding good from them, they took matters into their own hands, deciding to eat the fruit that was forbidden.

Most books on decision-making fail to factor in the significance of this one decision, which has eternal and lasting consequences on our own decision-making. In this single decision, the representatives of humanity severed vital relationship with God. As we make decisions today, significant aftershocks of Adam and Eve's decision still shake us. Before we think about the real and pressing decisions set before us, we are invited to remember Christ's decision to redeem us from the consequences of our choices.

The Drama of Redemption

Our decisions have depth. Some decisions, like what to order from Grubhub or which streaming service to use, stand on the surface of our lives. Other decisions, like which career path to follow or which person to marry, lie a stratum or two below. You likely picked up this book to address some of these questions, and I promise we will get to them. But first we will plumb the depths of our hearts to address our spiritual decisions. While the surface and middle-strata decisions are significant, the Scriptures tell the tale of humanity's poor spiritual choices.

Though we live in very different times and cultures from God's people in the Old and New Testaments, we share the same spiritual dilemma at the deepest level. Like them, even when God makes his commands clear, we fail to fulfill them. By sins of commission (wrong things done) and sins of omission (right things left undone), our spiritual choices have created a chasm between us and our God. In his letter to Titus, the apostle Paul perfectly sums up the broken system and the one who finally stepped in to fix it:

We ourselves were once foolish, disobedient, led astray, slaves to various passions and pleasures, passing our days in malice and envy, hated by others and hating one another. But when the goodness and loving kindness of God our Savior appeared, he saved us, not because of works done by us in righteousness, but according to his own mercy, by the washing of regeneration and renewal of the Holy Spirit, whom he poured out on us richly through Jesus Christ our Savior. (Titus 3:3–6)

God graciously decided to reconcile his people to himself. Predicting the coming of Christ through the Holy Spirit, Isaiah wrote, "Truth is lacking. . . . The LORD saw it, and it displeased him that there was no justice. He saw that there was no man, and wondered that there was no one to intercede; then his own arm brought him salvation, and his righteousness upheld him" (Isa. 59:15–16). Using poetic language of a warrior getting ready for battle, Isaiah describes Christ getting ready to come and bring salvation to his decision-decimated people. He wrote, "He put on righteousness as a breastplate, and a helmet of salvation on his head; he put on garments of vengeance for clothing, and wrapped himself in zeal as a cloak" (Isa. 59:17).

Christ, the second person of the Trinity, was born into time and space. Being fully man and fully God, he perfectly made his decisions under the gaze of his heavenly father. As the second Adam, he perfectly did what the first Adam had failed to do. Just as the curse entered the world through Adam's poor decision, salvation entered the world through Jesus's life of God-honoring decisions (Rom. 5:12–21).

In the great exchange that took place on the cross of Christ, God made the sinless one to bear the consequences of every wrong decision made by his children (2 Cor. 5:21). In the life, death, and resurrection of Christ, believers regain the ability to make decisions that will please God. In Christ, we are no longer judged on the sum of our disobedient decisions but on the sum of his obedient decisions. From that secured standing before God, we are invited into living lives that please him, decision by decision. In sending the Holy Spirit, the third person of the Trinity, to indwell the hearts of those who believe in him, Christ has given us a live-in guide in our decision-making.

The Drama of Decision-Making

Christ's finished work invites believers into the drama of decision-making. As his image bearers, we have freedom to make decisions that honor God. Through the indwelling Spirit who illuminates the word of God to make it understandable to us, we have been given all we need to make decisions with the mind of Christ (1 Cor. 2:16).

In Christ, we pick up where Adam and Eve failed. We're able to make decisions that honor God and advance his ways on earth. We have great freedom in the decisions we make, provided they do not go against his revealed word or quench the Spirit who indwells us, which we will address in subsequent chapters. God created us to be his children, not robots. As such, God extends to us the incredible and often weighty compliment of being decision makers.

In *The Screwtape Letters*, a fictional book of letters written from a senior demon to a young demon, C. S. Lewis depicts the demons as utterly confused as to why God, referred to as "the Enemy," would allow free will in his creatures:

> You must have often wondered why the Enemy does not make more use of His power to be sensibly present to human souls in any degree He chooses and at any moment. But you now see that the Irresistible and the Indisputable are the two weapons which the very nature of His scheme forbids Him to use. Merely to override a human will (as His felt presence in any but the faintest and most mitigated degree would certainly do) would be for Him useless. He cannot ravish. He can only woo.[3]

We may imagine life would be easier if God were to write out his will in the clouds or send a full blueprint of his plans for us. But when we wish for a simpler approach to decision-making, we ask for less than God intends for us. He would have us grow into mature sons and daughters who learn to make decisions through apprenticeship to him. Through his Spirit and his word, he will gradually form us into the kind of people who use their free will to obey, honor, and advance his ways. While a long and messy process, this glorifies him and affirms our dignity as his unique image bearers.

Before we move on in our discussion about the decision-making process, we are invited to stop and kneel before one of the many profound mysteries of the Christian faith.

God's Sovereignty and Man's Responsibility

Given that God is infinite, inexhaustible, unlimited, and eternal in his very nature, our attempts to understand him and his ways in the world are marked by a necessary mystery. The Christian life is riddled with mysteries that our finite minds struggle to comprehend. Our God is three in one, one in three. Jesus Christ was fully God and fully man. We are righteous in Christ and being made righteous simultaneously.

God, speaking through the prophet Isaiah, tells his people that his thoughts are not their thoughts, and his ways are not their ways. Just as the heavens are higher than the earth, God's ways are much higher than ours (Isa. 55:8–9). In his classic book *The Pursuit of God*, A. W. Tozer powerfully captures how we ought to respond when we bump into the mysteries of God. He writes, "The believing man does not claim to understand. He falls to his knees and whispers, 'God.'"[4]

When we approach the topic of God's will, we have to acknowledge the mystery of God's sovereignty and man's responsibility. When we face mysteries like these, we often find ourselves leaning heavily toward one side or the other. However, we do so at the peril of truth. If we lean too heavily on the side of man's responsibility, we will crush ourselves under the weight of decisions. Without the balancing and buoying reality of God's sovereignty, thousands of possibilities and potential consequences will paralyze us. Indeed, the overwhelming statistics of anxiety and depression gripping our world give evidence that we are leaning too heavily on man's responsibility. Without the knowledge of a good God who, in the words of Martin Luther, sovereignly draws straight with crooked sticks, decisions can lead to crippling fear and debilitating anxiety.

On the other hand, if we lean too heavily on God's sovereignty, we erroneously depict God as a puppeteer. We imagine him moving the strings to do what pleases him while we sit powerlessly pulled in various directions. This line of thinking, left unchecked by the balancing reality of our responsibility as image bearers, can quickly lead to fatalism and nihilism.

In his book *Evangelism and the Sovereignty of God*, J. I. Packer addresses the mystery of God's sovereignty and man's responsibility. He uses the long-disputed scientific debate over the nature of light to help us understand this *antimony*, which is "an apparent incompatibility between two apparent truths."[5] As physics was developing, some scientists and experiments proved, beyond the shadow of a doubt, that light behaved as a wave. Other scientists and experiments proved, beyond the shadow of a doubt, that light behaved as a particle. Both sides were certain that only one could be true, but both were wrong. Light is both wave and particle at the same time.

Packer continues to describe the antinomy between God's sovereignty, represented by God as king, and man's responsibility, represented by God as judge. Both are scripturally supported, sometimes in the same passage. He concludes, "Man is a responsible moral agent, though he is divinely controlled; man is divinely controlled, though he is also a responsible moral agent."[6]

We are free to make decisions, and those decisions matter. At the same time, our God is sovereign over every action and consequence, directing all human history toward his desired ends. Both are true simultaneously. While our human minds want to reconcile this antinomy, C. H. Spurgeon reminds us, "I never reconcile friends."[7] Rather than seeking to reconcile them, we are invited to kneel in awe before the God who holds all things together (Ps. 95:6; Col. 1:17). Elisabeth Elliot shows us how by stating, "Next to the Incarnation, I know of no more staggering and humbling truth than that a sovereign God has ordained my participation."[8]

Now that we have knelt in wonder and worship at the mystery of God's sovereignty and man's responsibility, we can continue to press forward in learning about our part in biblical decision-making.

2

The Design of Decisions

CITRUS TREES GROW IN ABUNDANCE in Southern California. When our family moved here from the Southeast, we decided to plant a dwarf blood orange tree in our front yard. With great decorum, I lugged my own human nursery of toddlers to the local tree nursery. We then proceeded to make quite a morning out of picking out the perfect tree. We planted our little sapling hoping for a fruitful spring, only to watch the poor thing struggle. We watered it regularly, talked to it, fertilized it, and waited. And waited. And waited.

Finally, about three years later, the tree began to bear fruit. While our blood orange tree is not the fruit-producing wonder we anticipated, it is *our* tree. We delight in gathering its moderate fruit, and we eat its fresh slices with great satisfaction. I could very easily head to Trader Joe's and purchase a bag of blood oranges; however, the process of growing and nurturing our own tree makes its scarce fruits even more precious.

In much the same way, God could have created an easier system for his children to arrive at decisions. He could have established a fortune-cookie system or given each of his children a Magic 8-Ball to consult. However, in his sovereign wisdom he preferred a relational, organic process. He invites us to search our own hearts and desires. He looks forward to spending time with us as we wrestle toward decisions. In his economy, both process and product are significant.

In the process of making decisions, we can fixate on the product or even the desired clarity; however, God enjoys the entire process in which we learn to trust him as children. I have watched multiple mentors walk their teenagers through the college application process. They spend countless hours coaxing, coaching, and correcting their children through the long and arduous process. Though it would be much easier to spin a wheel to select a college, the process provides yet another opportunity for them to deepen their existing relationships with their children.

Processes necessarily involve waiting. Waiting often involves tears and discomfort. The human heart in its fallen state does not like waiting. This reality is only exacerbated in an Amazon Prime culture accustomed to quick delivery. However, God's people have always been a waiting and wrestling people. Abraham and Sarah waited for their promised child for decades (Gen. 12–17). Joseph waited in prison for the cupbearer to remember him (Gen. 41). God's people, enslaved in Egypt, cried out and waited for a deliverer (Ex. 1–2). Later, God's exiled people waited to return home. After hearing the last words from the prophet Malachi, God's people waited over four hundred years to hear from another prophet. On the other side of the life, death, and resurrection of Christ, God's people continue to eagerly await his return (Rev. 22:7).

The process of making decisions, particularly significant ones, teaches us to wait as we wrestle. Such waiting and wrestling provide ample opportunities to look to the Lord. The decision-making process stretches our waiting muscles and helps us to look beyond our current situations to the ultimate end, the second coming of Christ.

Weighty decisions have a way of humbling us and exposing our limitations. Even though we have done the research and made an extensive list of pros and cons, we realize that we do not know what is best. We are limited in our understanding. We cannot see the future. In Psalm 131 we watch David wrestle as he waits upon the Lord for an answer. In the first verse, we find David in a humble posture before God, saying, "My heart is not lifted up; my eyes are not raised too high; I do not occupy myself with things too great and too marvelous for me" (Ps. 131:1). In the very next verse David beautifully displays a posture of trusting the Lord during the process: "But I have calmed and quieted my soul, like a weaned child with its mother; like a weaned child is my soul within me" (131:2). Despite being humbled and unsure within himself, David understands that his hope comes from the Lord who knows all things (131:3).

Whatever the situation that compelled you to read this book, God intends to use it to cultivate your ability to wait in humble dependence upon him. In a culture obsessed with product but impatient with process, God's people are invited into the purposeful process of decision-making alongside him. Our hope does not come from the process or the product but the God who lovingly directs both.

Intimacy through Process

When I think about people who allowed hard decisions to draw them further into intimacy with God, two unlikely biblical figures come to mind: Jehoshaphat and Mary.

Jehoshaphat served as king of Judah during a time of great strife, both within the divided kingdoms of God's people and without. In one instance, a group of neighboring nations arranged themselves in battle against him and his people. Jehoshaphat received a frantic report that a great multitude was coming against him. As the leader of his vulnerable people, Jehoshaphat felt the weight of significant decisions. His immediate, visceral response to a grim report instructs us as we seek to make our own decisions.

The writer of Chronicles records that Jehoshaphat "was afraid and set his face to seek the LORD, and proclaimed a fast throughout all Judah" (2 Chron. 20:3). After calling a nationwide fast, Jehoshaphat gathered the people together and led them in the following prayer:

> O LORD, God of our fathers, are you not God in heaven? You rule over all the kingdoms of the nations. In your hand are power and might, so that none is able to withstand you. . . . We do not know what to do, but our eyes are on you. (2 Chron. 20:6, 12)

No matter what decision is before us, we can take our cues from this ancient king, who laid out both the situation and his heart before God. We can choose to make the decision at hand our glance while gazing longer upon the God who will faithfully direct his humbled people.

Many centuries later, a young woman engaged to be married faced an unexpected decision of enormous weight. After being greeted by the angel Gabriel himself, she was told that God had chosen her to bear a son who would be called "the Son of the Most High" (Luke 1:32). Any decision to have a child is already weighty, so imagine the weight of considering carrying the promised Messiah! Mary, though understandably confused and overwhelmed, took a humble posture like Jehoshaphat. The physician Luke records her saying, "Behold, I am the servant of the Lord; let it be to me according to your word" (Luke 1:38).

Both Mary and Jehoshaphat allowed the process of decision-making to lead them further into intimacy, knowledge, and dependence upon the God whom they served. Rather than rush into decisions, both lingered in the presence of God and allowed him to shape their decisions.

Perplexed by Proverbs

Any search for practical wisdom in the Scriptures will likely pass through the book of Proverbs. After all, this book was intended, as Derek Kidner writes, to "put godliness into working clothes."[1] Written as instruction from father to son regarding practical life, the book of Proverbs "consists in the shrewd and sound handling of one's affairs in God's world, in submission to his will."[2] It is no surprise, then, that we would find ample proverbs regarding decision-making in the book of Proverbs, for godliness put into working clothes and placed into the real spheres of human life faces countless decisions. The proverbs teach us that wise men listen to counsel (Prov. 12:15), that the way that seems right is not always correct (Prov. 14:12), and that through the plans of a man, God's purpose will always have its way (Prov. 19:21). They instruct us to commit (literally roll) our plans and decisions onto the Lord (Prov. 16:3) rather than hold on to them tightly with grasping hands.

I remember spending hours in college puzzling over the proverbs that dealt with decision-making. As a senior biology major with a chemistry minor who had grown a passion for making disciples, I stood at a crossroad. Would I apply to medical school and spend countless hours in libraries and labs working toward a career in medicine? Or would I decide to raise financial support for vocational ministry, letting all those hours of anatomy and physiology, microbiology, and genetics gather dust on the shelf? A medical career would uniquely enable me to meet the physical needs of others as an avenue toward also meeting spiritual needs with the gospel. Clearly God would be for that! But at the same time, God would be pleased with me raising financial support to be freed to minister to college students spiritually. Clearly God would be for that as well! Both would have been good options pleasing to the Lord. Both were competing plans in my heart. Depending on the day (or even the minute) both seemed best in my own eyes.

I camped out in the book of Proverbs, hoping to find a particular proverb to the effect of, "The biology major who loves God will continue to medical school" or "Full-time ministry is a honeycomb of life." But I searched to no avail. I found, much to my chagrin, that decision-making is not a formula like the quadratic equation. Real-life career choices do not balance out neatly like stoichiometry. In the end, the Lord directed me to neither of the plans I had spent the better part of a year wrestling with. Instead, he opened doors for me to use my biology degree as a high school teacher. During that first year of teaching (more to come on that critical year in chapter 5), God redirected me toward vocational ministry in a way I had not anticipated—I ended up marrying a man called to college ministry.

The proverbs do not spell out a formula for decision-making. Such a formula does not exist, and even if it did, it would not engender the intimacy-producing and wisdom-developing process that God intends for his children. No matter how much we wish to the contrary, the Scriptures are unlikely to have a direct verse that clearly makes your decision for you. Instead God would have us, in real freedom, considering real wisdom, make real decisions that have real consequences. We seek God for answers, but God is far more interested in giving us more of himself.

Choices and Consequences

Decisions paralyze us precisely because we innately know that our choices have consequences. Decisions about where to live, whom to surround ourselves, and how to invest our finances have far-reaching consequences. Consequences are not intended to terrorize us but rather to train us. They teach us to become better decision makers.

If you are not convinced, ask any teacher about the significant role consequences play in the classroom. To become capable learners, students must learn that their choices have real consequences. Most teachers affirm that well-intended helicopter parents hinder development when they attempt to help. When parents step in to relieve students of the natural consequences of being unprepared for a test or beginning a project the night before the due date, they truncate necessary development. To help them in the present, they cripple them for the future. Consequences train decision makers.

In much the same way, God allows the natural consequences of our actions to shape and change us. He trains his children as those who will live eternally. Just as God wove physical laws into the fabric of the universe, God created spiritual laws that work similarly. The law of gravity regulates life on earth, whether you agree to it or not. It would be the height of all pride to announce, "I don't like gravity; therefore, it does not apply to me." Even as you announce your avowed disbelief, gravity would be holding you onto your soapbox. Likewise, when we planted our blood orange tree, we fully expected blood oranges to grow. Had it fruited apples, the laws of nature would have been broken.

In his letter to the Galatians Paul wrote, "Do not be deceived: God is not mocked, for whatever one sows, that will he also reap. For the one who sows to his own flesh will from the flesh reap corruption, but the one who sows to the Spirit will from the Spirit reap eternal life" (Gal. 6:7–8). In essence, Paul reminds the Jewish believers that spiritual choices have consequences. Paul is not saying something novel here; rather, he is speaking in accordance with principles that have played out throughout God's interaction with his people.

God listened to the desperate cries of his enslaved people and sent them a rescuer in Moses. However, shortly after their dramatic Red Sea rescue, God left them real choices with real consequences regarding the promised land. While the Israelites were not in escrow on the land, God promised he would give them the land of Canaan. They had every reason to believe he would. Only weeks before, they had witnessed the plagues, been spared by blood on their doorposts, and walked through the Red Sea (Ex. 7–12).

Yahweh had a growing record of trustworthiness and power. Yet God's people complained, doubted, and whined their way through the wilderness. Sustained by God's miraculous provision of manna, they walked toward the land that was promised them. As they got closer to the promised land, Moses sent select leaders to check it out. Upon their return, ten of the twelve spies gave reports that were processed through the lens of fear. The land was amazing. The clusters of grapes were so big that they had to be carried between poles by two men. But its inhabitants were larger than life. Their fearful perspective spread throughout the camp.

Caleb and Joshua had seen the same land as the other ten spies, only they saw it through eyes of faith rather than fear. They declared, "If the LORD delights in us, he will bring us into this land and give it to us, a land that flows with milk and honey" (Num. 14:8). The people trusted the ten fearful spies. In his mercy, God allowed them to live, but their choices would have serious consequences. None of the ten fearful spies would set foot in the promised land. Caleb and Joshua, on the other hand, entered the good land in their old age (Num. 14:20–25).

Twelve spies. The same task. The same land. The same facts. Different choices. Different consequences.

The consequences of our choices are real, but God's mercy and grace to us, even in those consequences, are also real. As you approach the decisions laid before you, remember the two spies who walked in obedient faith. However, as you sift through potential outcomes, also remember that our God cares about all suffering, even that which we bring upon ourselves.[3] Even in the midst of the dire consequences of their poor choices, God continued to feed his disobedient people with manna (Deut. 8:1–10).

Even though David was a man after God's own heart (1 Sam. 13:14), he made disastrous decisions. In two instances, David made poor choices with far-reaching consequences. Though these incidents occurred many years apart, both are tipped off by the phrase, "In the spring of the year, the time when kings go out to battle" (2 Sam. 11:1; 1 Chron. 20:1). Two of the greatest failures in David's life (his affair with Bathsheba and its subsequent murder plot, and a selfishly initiated census) began with simple, small choices that led down dangerous paths. Although David showed deep repentance and remorse, dire consequences still happened to him and even those around him. David and Bathsheba lost their child, and many Israelites were killed in a plague. However, even in meting out necessary consequences, we see hints of God's plan to perfectly satisfy his justice while honoring his lovingkindness.

After David's census, the angel of the Lord relented concerning the then-imminent destruction of Jerusalem (1 Chron. 21). He did so in full knowledge that one day another man after God's own heart would bear the full weight of the wrath of God. At the cross, God's perfect Son bore our consequences so that we might receive his unmerited grace (1 Pet. 2:24).

In order to move forward with the decisions we face, it helps us to understand God's ultimate design for the decision-making process. Having addressed God's design for our own choices and consequences, we will now explore God's providence in directing us even through the choices of others.

Providence and the Choices of Others

Life would be less messy if our lives were merely the result of our own choices; however, our lives are an intricate and elaborate web of our own choices and the choices of others. While modern culture tells us that we are the masters of our destinies, the complexity of our lives tells us differently. Whether we like it or not, our lives are deeply affected by factors outside of our control. We do not choose the families into which we are born, the genetics with which our bodies are woven, or the circumstances which set the stage for our lives. The reality that our lives are inextricably bound to the choices and consequences of others both sobers and scares us. Such a truth sometimes leads to feelings of powerlessness and hopelessness. Thankfully, the Scriptures offer hope for those feeling trapped by the decisions of others.

While the didactic portions of Scripture teach us biblical principles and the nature of our God, the narrative portions invite us to see these realities played out in the lives of people. God not only tells us about his providential care, but he also provides narratives that show us this care. The story of Joseph gives perspective to those whose lives are significantly shaped by others' choices.

We first meet Joseph in Genesis 37, when his jealous brothers conspire to kill him. By God's intervening mercy, they stop short, leaving him mangled in the wilderness. He is trapped internally by his brother's hatred and externally by the walls of a deep pit. However, as the story of Joseph plays out in the ensuing chapters of Genesis, the reader sees God's providential hand in the troubled life of Joseph. Midianite traders rescue Joseph and bring him to Egypt, where he rises to a high position in the household of Potiphar, a high-ranking Egyptian officer (Gen. 37–39).

Just when things seem to be looking up for Joseph, his life is once again profoundly impacted by the choices of another. When Potiphar's wife falsely accuses him of making advances at her, Joseph once again finds himself internally and externally imprisoned by the poor choices of others (Gen. 39:11–20). Yet throughout Joseph's life, God's providential hand provides, protects, and guides him. During all the trying circumstances, "the Lord was with Joseph" (Gen. 39:2, 5, 23). The story reaches its climax when Joseph comes to a critical choice in his own life. In Genesis 45, Joseph forgives his brothers, choosing to rescue those who had ravaged him. In the succinct phrase, "As for you, you meant evil against me, but God meant it for good" (Gen. 50:20), the writer of Genesis sums up the powerful reality of God's providential dealings with his people.

Joseph's story points to another Son whose life was powerfully shaped by others' choices. Unlike Joseph, Jesus chose the path laid before him. On the cross, Christ took upon himself the consequences we deserve. He took what we intend for evil and worked it for our great good. Through the life, death, and resurrection of Christ, God makes evident his good intentions for his children. The light of the gospel shines into the dark pits and prisons we experience due to the choices of others.

Healthy Fear

Fear often accompanies our decisions. While all fear is uncomfortable, not all fear is sinful. In fact, a better understanding of a healthy fear of God can serve as a trusted guide rather than an uninvited companion. Pastor Sinclair Ferguson makes a helpful distinction between servile fear and filial fear. The word *servile* comes from the Latin word meaning "slave," while the word *filial* comes from the Latin word meaning "son." Healthy Christian fear is "that indefinable mixture of reverence, fear, pleasure, joy and awe which fills our hearts when we realize who God is and what He has done for us."[4]

While servile fear makes us its slave, healthy Christian fear keeps us walking in the freedom of Christ. Filial fear reminds us that we make all our decisions *coram deo,* or "in the presence or before the face of God." Just as children are more apt to make wise choices in the presence of a trusted adult, healthy fear that we live *coram deo* instructs and informs our decisions. For the believer, all of life is lived under the gaze and authority of God (Prov. 15:3; Heb. 4:13). We live in the presence of the God in whom we live and move and have our being (Acts 17:38). Filial fear can powerfully shape the decisions that have us shaking with servile fear, constraining us to make decisions that honor our Father (Col. 1:10).

The gospel of grace does not negate the law of choice and consequence. In the gospel, we see the justice of God meting out circumstances fitting to our unfaithfulness to him. Christ took upon himself the punishment we deserve because of our choice to dethrone God. The apostle Paul succinctly writes that God "made him to be sin who knew no sin, so that in him we might become the righteousness of God" (2 Cor. 5:21).

Jesus voluntarily chose to take upon himself the consequences of our sin. This should cause us to stand in awe. Rather than decrease our fear of God regarding decision-making, it should increase our filial fear, that appropriate fear of sons and daughters adopted through the blood of the one faithful Son of God. The one who worked the ultimate good out of ultimate evil can work good out of our choices. Such a powerful truth sets our hearts at ease while simultaneously teaching us to stand in respectful attention. We make choices as chosen ones. His choice to step into time and set his face toward the cross informs our choices. When we remember that it was his choice to give himself up for us, despite our treacherous choices, we begin to see our daily decisions in a new light.

Problem or Privilege?

When we experience the fear and confusion that accompany decisions, the ability to make decisions can sometimes feel more like a problem than a privilege. The reality that God has equipped us to make important choices with lasting consequences can feel like a heavy weight. However, it is the weight of glory given to us as God's image bearers.

Before Jesus left his disciples, he sought to prepare them for their appointed purpose. They were rightly reluctant to have him depart through death. Having walked with him for three years, they did not want him to leave them. However, Christ promised them, "Whoever believes in me will also do the works that I do; and greater works than these will he do, because I am going to the Father" (John 14:12). Later, when Christ ascended to the Father, the disciples felt the weight of the kingdom. However, Christ sent the Holy Spirit as helper to empower them to do his work on earth.

God intends to multiply his works by multiplying his ambassadors and representatives on earth. When God redeems someone, he fully intends to shape that someone into the image of his Son. As C. S. Lewis put it:

> Now the whole offer which Christianity makes is this: that we can, if we let God have His way, come to share in the life of Christ. . . . If we share in this kind of life we also shall be sons of God. We shall love the Father as He does and the Holy Ghost will arise in us.[5]

While justification is the beginning of new life in Christ, sanctification is the invitation to grow in having the mind of Christ (1 Cor. 2:16). Rather than giving us a formula for decision-making, God has instituted a relational process by which his adopted children more fully become like their Father. As we grow in Christlikeness through intimacy with God and Spirit-enabled obedience to his word, we are increasingly able to think, act, and decide with the mind of Christ. God multiplies his presence on earth even through us. Our decisions can help usher in the kingdom of God here and now, that his will might be done on earth as it is in heaven.

3

Theological Foundations for Decisions

ONCE A YEAR, my family and I put on our baseball hats, hop on the trolley, and head to downtown San Diego to attend a Padres game. At some point during the event, the three-cup game appears on the screen, bidding the fans to figure out which of three constantly moving cups hides a ball. No matter how hard I try, I cannot win the game. The frantic movement of the three cups leaves me dizzy and confused.

When most of us think about decision-making and God's will, we sometimes feel as if God were playing the three-cup game with us. While we are right to assume that God has a will for our lives, we can wrongly assume that God is playing a game with us. We erroneously think we must wrestle God's will from his hands. We fear that we will somehow miss his will or that we will have to settle for a plan B. I cannot tell you how many times I have heard college students, recent graduates, and even adult friends agonizing in fear that they somehow "missed" God's will for their lives. Such thinking betrays that we would be served by a careful study of the use of the term "God's will" in Scripture.

God's Will

Before we can make decisions, it is helpful to have a robust biblical understanding of the nature of God's will. When we think about God's will, most of us think immediately about his will regarding specific decisions we are facing. We want to know whether it is God's will that we become a doctor. We desire to know if this specific person is the one God intends to be our spouse. We wonder whether we should buy this stock or that bond. These are significant questions, and I promise we will get to them. However, as a starting point, it is instructive to know that biblical references to God's will most often pertain to (1) his eternal plans and decrees, (2) what is favorable to him, and (3) his providential guidance. It is difficult to draw firm distinctions between these three, as they are braided tightly together. Yet in order to gain a better understanding of God's will, we will attempt to broadly identify each strand.

We see God's will referring to "his eternal, sovereign rulership over the world" concisely in the words of King Nebuchadnezzar that are recorded in Daniel 4.[1] As king of Babylon, Nebuchadnezzar knew a thing or two about decrees. After all, what he declared and decreed became law in his land. Yet after witnessing the power of the God of Israel, Nebuchadnezzar realized that there was one far more powerful than himself.

I blessed the Most High, and praised and honored him who lives forever,

for his dominion is an everlasting dominion,
    and his kingdom endures from generation to
        generation;
all the inhabitants of the earth are counted as nothing,
    and he does according to his will among the host of
        heaven
    and among the inhabitants of the earth;
and none can stay his hand
    or say to him, "What have you done?" (Dan. 4:34–35)

Likewise the pharaoh of Egypt, another one familiar with power and decrees, saw God's greater will on display through the plagues (Ex. 7–12). However, we need not be kings, queens, or powerful rulers to understand the power of God's sovereignty over all human history. Scripture is replete with powerful examples of our powerful King of kings and Lord of lords (Job 38–40; Ps. 104; Isa. 40:21–26).

Another way we can think of God's will is "what He wants and what is favorable to Him."[2] Speaking of God's desire that his people not be destroyed, despite their sin, Moses said, "The LORD was unwilling to destroy you" (Deut. 10:10). Just as earthly parents do not prefer pain for their children, God did not want his people to be destroyed. In the New Testament, the apostle Paul uses the Greek word translated "will" in a similar way. Like many modern believers, believers in the church at Thessalonica were wrestling over decisions. Paul responded to their confusion, saying, "This is the will of God, your sanctification" (1 Thess. 4:3). Here, Paul concisely claimed that God's deep desire is that his people be conformed to his image. We will further discuss this reality later in this chapter because it has widespread implications for our daily lives.

God's will can also refer to divine providence. While this term, *providence*, is thrown around in secular circles as a synonym for fate or luck, for the believer in Christ it refers to God's sovereign care for and ordering of his world and his people. Chapter 5 of the Westminster Confession of Faith defines providence as follows:

> God, the great Creator of all things, doth uphold, direct, dispose, and govern all creatures, actions, and things, from the greatest to the least, by his most wise and holy providence, according to his infallible foreknowledge, and the free and immutable counsel of his own will, to the praise of the glory of his wisdom, power, justice, goodness, and mercy.[3]

Contrary to popular belief, God's providential plan for our lives does not mean that we are mere pawns in his hands. His providence is an expression of his imminence and involvement in the lives of the humans he has created. As A. W. Tozer says, "The unbeliever cries, 'I am God's pawn!' The believer sings, 'I am God's beloved.'"[4]

God's providential dealings with us can only be seen backwards in the rearview mirror after we have walked in wisdom, faith, and obedience. It's only after you've taken that job, made that move, or married that sweetheart that you discover these things were God's providential care for you. You can't declare his providence in advance, but you can see it displayed in hindsight. God invites us to walk by faith, in the assurance of things hoped for and the conviction of things unseen (Heb. 11:1). Looking back on our lives, we will be able to trace his providential dealings with us; however, we waste our time if we try to discern his providences before they happen (Gen. 45:5, 7, 8; 2 Cor. 12:7–9). Even though we cannot see his providence until we are looking back, we can live in confidence that our God is always guiding us with his providential care. He is near and actively engaged in ordering all of history in nations, neighborhoods, and even the necessary decisions of our individual days.

God's Will in Specific Situations

In a few cases, the term *will* refers to God's specific choice in a complex situation. Like us, God's people wanted to know his will in practical situations. *Should we go up against this army? How long should we camp out here? Who should be our king?* God, being both gracious and revelatory, seeks to guide his people. Before the coming of Christ, the Holy Spirit was actively involved in guiding God's people. When God's people were leaving Egypt, a pillar of cloud and fire led them, telling them where to go and how long to remain in each place (Ex. 13:21–22; Ps. 105:39). Also, in Exodus 28, God provided a temporary method by which the priests could seek the Lord's will for specific situations. The Urim and the Thummim were instruments held near the heart within the breastplate of the priest (Ex. 2:30; Lev. 8:8). While scholars are not certain exactly how they were used to provide yes or no answers, we know that they were a gracious provision by which the leaders were able to seek God's direction.[5]

Even with these provisions, saints in the Old Testament most often made decisions in the same way we do today. They gathered the facts, they prayed and sought the Lord, and they wrestled and waited. While Hannah was barren, she prayed and begged God to provide her a child. Using the means available, she and her husband Elkanah sacrificed and prayed, brought their burden to the appointed priests, and continued forward in faith (1 Sam. 1). No special means were used to determine if it was God's will that she bear a son. They walked by faith in what they knew of God's character. While Abraham did receive an initial call from God himself, most of his years of walking to an unknown destination and waiting for a promised son were marked by wrestling and praying to trust God based on what God had revealed about himself. It wasn't all burning bushes for Moses either. While he certainly had some mountaintop experiences, he also had seasons of listening to trusted counselors, gathering the facts, and making judicial decisions to the best of his ability through the natural wisdom allotted to him by God (Ex. 18).

If you are like me, you have hoped God would guide and direct you through the clearer, supernatural means. When agonizing between two job offers, I wanted God to simply write the answer in the sky. When I first began walking with Christ in high school, I knew nothing about Scripture. I essentially trusted God to guide me through the open-and-point method. I would randomly flip through pages of the Precious Moments Bible given to me at birth. Eventually, I would pick a page and point, hoping whatever random verse my finger landed on would provide the wisdom needed. While God does occasionally condescend to use these means (as he did in the conversion of Augustine), God intends that we learn his full counsel. We are invited to read, meditate upon, and study the word of God until it begins to dye and stain our souls in his likeness.

Part of me wishes I could sit down with Moses to ask him about being led by the pillars of cloud and fire. I would love to ask Aaron what it was like to wield the Urim and Thummim. However, I think both Moses and Aaron would want to interview saints who live on the other side of the life of Christ. For them, the reality of the Holy Spirit indwelling the saints would be astounding! As Christ declared in his eulogy for his cousin John the Baptist, "Truly, I say to you, among those born of women there has arisen no one greater than John the Baptist. Yet the one who is least in the kingdom of heaven is greater than he" (Matt. 11:11). Those are strong words from the Savior, yet they remind us of the unthinkable privilege of being the temple of the Holy Spirit (1 Cor. 6:19–20).

In a world laced with decisions, from the minute to the monumental, we deeply desire to know God's will for the situations and circumstances of our lives. However, we will not find God's will using the Urim and Thummim. As much as we may wish that God would send an actual pillar of fire to lead us through life's crossroads, God has given us something better. After the coming of Christ, these unique means of revealing his specific choice in complex situations were no longer necessary. Such methods of discerning God's will were temporary provisions to guide and direct his people. As shadows are to substance, these means pale in comparison to what God intends for us as we make decisions today. We have something far better in the third person of the Trinity. He works in us to conform us to the likeness of Christ (2 Cor. 3:16–18), to develop in us the mind of Christ (1 Cor. 2:14), and to guide us into the works that God has prepared beforehand that we might walk in them (Eph. 2:10). While we still have some of the methods used in the Old Testament to make wise decisions (seeking counsel, praying, fasting), we now also have the Holy Spirit who lives within us to comfort us, convict us, and illuminate the Scriptures to us.

God is a good Father who provides for and protects his children. He is a good shepherd who delights to lead his flock to green pastures and away from dangers (Ps. 23; Luke 12:32; John 10:10–11). We may wish that decision-making was more formulaic or less confusing. I know I do! Yet God has something far more relational, intimate, and involved than cloud-writing or casting lots. He trusts us to use the wisdom he has given us and placed within us, the body of Christ, and the minds he has wired within us to make real decisions in real time with real consequences. As we make decisions and experience their resultant consequences, we will grow in maturity and dependence upon him. He intends to increasingly form us into his image and likeness. In the poetic words of George Herbert, "But can he want the grape, who hath the wine?"[6]

He has given us his incarnate Word in the form of his Son (John 1). He has entrusted to us his revealed word through the canonical Scriptures (2 Tim. 3:16–17). He has chosen to make his home in us through the third person of the Trinity. He has given us great, though often frustrating, freedom. As we discussed in the first chapter, he did not create us as automatons but as his image bearers. He is jealous for our affection, our attention, and our dependence. As such, we are invited into the relational process of decision-making.

Hidden and Revealed Will

Having explored the wide range of biblical meaning for the term "will of God," it may be helpful to consider a simplified way of approaching God's will. It is helpful to divide God's will into two categories: his revealed will and his hidden will. God's revealed will for us is found in his word, while God's hidden will, as implied in the name, is hidden and cannot be known until we are able to look back on it.

God's word reveals all we need to know about God's will. As Peter so powerfully reminded the early church, God's precious and very great promises provide all we need for life and godliness (2 Pet. 1:3–4). The apostle Paul, facing an impending death at the hands of Emperor Nero, reminded his young protégé and successor Timothy the significance of the Scriptures in the life of those who are seeking to live for Christ. He reminded his friend that the Scriptures were breathed out by God and are "profitable for teaching, for reproof, for correction, and for training in righteousness, that the man of God may be complete, equipped for every good work" (2 Tim. 3:16–17). Similarly, the writer of Hebrews reminded the earliest Jewish believers that the word of God was no mere book, but rather "living and active, sharper than any two-edged sword, piercing to the division of soul and of spirit, of joints and of marrow, and discerning the thoughts and intentions of the heart" (Heb. 4:12).

Even though we have the revealed will of God in his word, many of us want to know more of his hidden will. Author Jerry Sittser expresses the frustration which so many of us experience regarding the hidden parts of God's will:

The Bible is frustrating clear on some matters about which we want to know little, and opaque on other matters about which we want to know much. It tells us what we must do today, for example, which often involves mundane tasks we tend to over-look. It tells us precious little about what is going to happen tomorrow, except to say that God is in control. . . . It is positively loquacious concerning what God wants us to do today; it is virtually mum about what God has in store for us tomorrow.[7]

From our limited vantage point as time-bound, finite crea-tures, we cannot know the future. The length of days we each have on this earth and what will happen tomorrow are part of God's hidden will. While this may initially sound defeating, it is helpful to consider all that we *do* know about God's revealed will is in his word. We don't know *where* we will live in five years, but we do know *how* we are to live. We may not know if we will marry or whom we will marry, but we do know God wills that we avoid sexual immorality and marry someone with a similar love for Christ (Eph. 5:3; 2 Cor. 6:14–15). We may not know if our entrepreneurial business venture will be successful, but we know God's will is for us to conduct our business uprightly and to trust him in plenty or in want (Prov. 16:11; Phil. 4:11–13). We may not know which neighborhood or country we will live in, but we do know from God's revealed will that he intends we love and serve our neighbors (Mark 12:28–31).

In Deuteronomy 29:29 Moses reminds the often wandering hearts of his wandering people, "The secret things belong to the Lord our God, but the things that are revealed belong to us and to our children forever, that we may do all the words of this law." Here, Moses makes a similar distinction between the secret things and the revealed words of God. How similar we are to the wander-ing Israelites, constantly wanting to peer into the secret things!

We want to know the origin of evil, to see the full blueprint of our lives laid out before us, and to understand things he never intended for us to understand here on earth. However, God has lovingly determined what is necessary for us to live our lives according to his purpose and his plan. Being a good Father, he has given us all that we need to know him and make him known on our pilgrimage on earth.

In his book *Knowing God*, J. I. Packer talks about the way we tend to imagine God offering us wisdom and the way he actually offers it. Using two different transport analogies, he juxtaposes a train yard and learning to drive. We wish God's wisdom was like being offered a personal tour of the railroad signal box. We desire "deepened insight into the providential meaning and purpose of events going on around us, an ability to see why God has done what He has done in a particular case, and what He is going to do next."[8] However, God does not offer us this type of wisdom. Rather, when God offers us wisdom, he allows us to see the road as it unfolds before us, as one driving a car. When driving a car, we shouldn't be thinking about why the road turns left or right or why the car next to us is blue or red. "You try to see and do the right thing in the actual situation that presents itself."[9]

While God is large enough to invite our wonder, our curiosity, and our questions, he has fully provided the truths we need to honor him with our decisions. He welcomes our musing and mulling over the things we don't understand, but he commands us to live in view of what he has clearly revealed in his word. While there is much we won't understand until we are face-to-face with Christ, there is so much that we do know this side of glory (1 Cor. 13:12). God commands us to walk by faith, making decisions that align with his revealed will until we can know his hidden will (Heb. 11:6).

We waste the precious time allotted to us when we seek to find out the hidden things in the decision-making process. He would have us walk by faith in his revealed will and entrust to him the hidden things. After all, they are much safer in his sovereign hands. When we begin to wrestle and doubt, it is helpful to remember that we can know God's intentions and will for us most clearly through the incarnation of his Son. To that end, Paul rhetorically asks, "He who did not spare his own Son but gave him up for us all, how will he not also with him graciously give us all things?" (Rom. 8:32).

Rather than seeking to curiously peer into his hidden will, we are invited to chase after his righteousness (Matt. 6:33). As we walk in alignment with God's revealed will, we can trust his hidden will to unfold as God has planned since before there was time. Jerry Sittser expresses the comfort we find in knowing and seeking to obey God's revealed will:

> If we seek first God's kingdom and righteousness, which is the will of God for our lives, then whatever choices we make concerning the future become the will of God for our lives. There are many pathways we could follow, many options we could pursue. As long as we are seeking God, all of them can be God's will for our lives, although only one—the path we choose—actually becomes his will.[10]

We tend to spend so much time agonizing over all the potential paths we could take that we often overlook what God cares most about. He cares less which path we choose and far more how and why we choose it. Whether you become a teacher or a doctor, he cares more about the kind of doctor or teacher you are becoming. He cares far more about what is going on within the walls of your house than about the colors of your walls or the specifics of your address. He cares more about the way you love your neighbors than the neighborhood you live in.

It will take all the days we've been allotted and all the strength we have been given through the Holy Spirit to live in accordance with God's revealed will. Such a task is the worthy endeavor, as there is much to learn about God through his word. We are invited to spend the rest of our lives walking in his truth. As we seek to understand and apply God's word to our lives, we will quickly learn our need for discernment even within the revealed things.

The Three Types of Law

When it comes to matters of straightforward obedience, the only decision to be made is whether to walk in Spirit-empowered, trusting obedience or to walk by the flesh and so gratify the desires of the flesh (Gal. 5:16–17). However, the revealed word contains three different types of law: ceremonial law, civil law, and moral law. It is necessary to have a general understanding of these three types of law so we can make clear distinctions about which commands God still intends for his people to obey today.

Anyone who has attempted to read through the Bible in a year likely stalled out for some time in the book of Leviticus, where considerable time is spent exploring ceremonial law. Ceremonial law was given to regulate the sacrificial system and covered such things as handwashing, temple worship, and which animals were to be sacrificed. However, the entire elaborate sacrificial system was always intended to point to Christ, the perfect sacrifice. The writer of Hebrews powerfully juxtaposes for Jewish believers the sacrificial system established in the old covenant with the once-for-all sacrifice of Christ, the perfect sacrifice who ushered in the new covenant with his blood:

> When Christ had offered for all time a single sacrifice for sins, he sat down at the right hand of God, waiting from that time until his enemies should be made a footstool for his feet. For by a single offering he has perfected for all time those who are being sanctified. (Heb. 10:12–14)

Therefore, all the ceremonial law is ultimately fulfilled in Christ. There is no need for any additional sacrifices for sin because Christ's blood is sufficient for all. You no longer must seek cleansing in the temple after touching a dead body, completing your menstrual cycle, or having a baby. Thankfully, you don't have to fast on the day of atonement or kill two pigeons at Passover. All these things are part of the ceremonial law, which Christ completely fulfilled.

A second type of law, the civil law, was intended to help direct the nation of Israel as God's set-apart people. These laws, which included restitution for stolen ox or sheep and laws about social justice, governed God's people as a growing nation. While God's focus throughout the Old Testament was Israel, God's scope was always the nations. Having sent his son into the Jewish line of David, God shows his people that the kingdom of God was something altogether different and better than an actual nation.[11]

When the Gentiles were invited into the gospel, the civil laws that were intended to govern God's people as a theocracy became obsolete. While we may glean some of the principles that undergirded the old civil laws, we are no longer bound to follow them to the letter (Heb. 8:13).

The moral law shows us what life in the Spirit looks like and is summarized in shorthand form in the Ten Commandments. While Jesus was on earth, he himself said, "Do not think that I have come to abolish the Law or the Prophets; I have not come to abolish them but to fulfill them" (Matt. 5:17). Far from negating the Ten Commandments, Christ revealed the fullness God had always intended by them. Whereas the Pharisees had narrowed God's laws to make them seem more easily doable, Christ showed the full extent of God's intention. While the religious teachers focused on outward acts, Christ addressed the heart beneath such outward actions. Thus he showed murder to include much more than the act of killing another. He connected murderous actions to anger in our hearts toward another. He similarly addressed adultery and covetousness, regaining the internal ground of the heart that had been ignored by the religious teachers' whittling God's commandments down to something more measurable. God wants much more than behavior modification. He would have his people transformed from the inside out.

Long ago, the prophet Ezekiel hinted that God intended for his law to be written on the tablets of human hearts rather than on tablets of stone (Ezek. 36:26–27; see also Jer. 31:33; 2 Cor. 3:3). Believers on the other side of the life, death, and resurrection of Christ are those of whom Ezekiel spoke. We who are indwelt by the Spirit see clearly what Ezekiel saw in fuzzy forms. Christ, who perfectly fulfilled and embodied the moral law, sent the Spirit to live in us. The same Spirit transforms us into those who seek to keep and embody the moral law.

As those who look back on the cross, we are free to enjoy pork and shellfish (civil laws that no longer apply to the new covenant). We no longer must procure perfect, spotless lambs to atone for our failures (ceremonial laws fulfilled and set aside in Christ). Our life in Christ frees us from the condemnation of the moral law (Rom. 8:1–2), but it also frees and equips us to live Christlike lives that increasingly embody the moral law (Gal. 5:13; 1 Pet. 2:16; 1 John 5:3). God's Spirit within us will always direct us to keep the moral law. While only Christ perfectly fulfilled the moral law, this reality should free us to strive for Christlikeness.

A proper understanding of the three types of biblical law helps to clear up many false dilemmas. I cannot tell you how many times I have had conversations with friends who were torn up about decisions on whether to live with a girlfriend or boyfriend, whether to join friends in underaged drinking, or whether to include income on their tax return. The only decision for the believer in Christ in these cases is whether they will obey or disobey the moral laws God has clearly laid out in his word.

Simplicity and Complexity in God's Revealed Will

Now that we understand the three types of law, we are better equipped to understand which parts of God's revealed will directly apply to our lives today. However, even within the moral law, there are times when God's revealed will is pointed and specific and times when his revealed will is more complex and its application more nuanced.

For example, the seventh commandment clearly prohibits adultery (Ex. 20:14). As such, extramarital affairs, whether emotional or physical, are always wrong, no matter how strongly you feel the emotions of love or how you might seek to justify it in your flesh (James 1:14–15). There is little room for Christian liberty or nuance here. However, other commands within God's revealed will, though equally clear, are more complex in their application and leave room for greater Christian liberty. The fifth commandment clearly commands believers to honor mother and father (Ex. 20:12). While this command is equally clear, its application can be diverse depending on one's family of origin, cultural context, and present circumstances. My husband and I have sought to honor our parents, which also includes caring well for them as they age. Yet at the same time, God has called us to minister in Southern California, far away from both our families of origin. While some families honor their parents by bringing them to live in their home, we must honor and provide for our parents from a distance. In situations in which the revealed will of God leaves room for nuanced and varying application and decisions, believers are invited to walk in the way of wisdom.

Moving beyond the simple and complex (or specific and general) commands in the revealed will of God, our lives will lead us into topics and decisions about which the Scriptures are unclear or silent. According to the Westminster Confession of Faith, God leaves the believer's conscience open in matters of human preferences that go beyond what Scripture dictates.[12] In the days of the early church, the eating of meats sacrificed to idols fell into this category (1 Cor. 10:14–33). In our present context, questions about how to vote in elections, which schools to attend, and how to view alcohol would fall into this category.[13] While God most assuredly cares that his children's minds be formed, he allows great liberty for each family to decide between homeschool, private school, or public school. While God's word clearly speaks against drunkenness, individual believers are given liberty to decide whether to imbibe alcohol lawfully or not (Gal. 5:19–21; Eph. 5:19).

In the next few chapters we will address tools and principles to help us make God-honoring decisions both in areas of complexity and areas of Christian liberty. Just as a house's foundation, while unseen, provides the necessary stability for all that is built upon it, our labor to lay a sturdy theological foundation now allows us to proceed into the more practical side of the decision-making process.

4

The Dashboard of Decisions

SINCE HIS TEENS, a dear friend of mine has always dreamed of flying planes. In the past few years he began takings steps to make his dreams a reality, taking courses, logging flight hours, and poring over textbooks, inching toward his private and commercial licenses. Apparently, flight is far more complex than buckling a seatbelt and putting a tray table in its upright and locked position. Pilots gather information from an entire dashboard of complex gauges as they make in-flight decisions. As we make decisions, we, too, have complex dashboards with gauges consciously and subconsciously directing us.

At the center of our proverbial dashboard sits the God gauge. As noted in previous chapters, all humans are wired for connection with their Creator God. We were created by him and for him; however, in the catastrophic moment known as the fall, our forefather and foremother cut its wiring, disconnecting humanity from its source. Unless one is reconnected to God through salvation, this crucial gauge sits dark and unused.

Other significant gauges—a cultural gauge, an idolatry gauge, a desire gauge, and an urgency gauge—litter the dashboard, each providing important information that is used to make an informed decision. Depending on one's family of origin, shaping circumstances, and personality, these gauges grow or shrink in their significance in the decision-making process. Familiarizing ourselves with gauges may sound about as exciting as a field trip to the hardware aisle at Home Depot. However, the knowledge we glean from these gauges might mean the difference between a fulfilling job we look forward to daily and a job we dislike. Identifying the impulses and voices informing our decisions might save us from things like settling into a marriage of convenience or from buying a house in a neighborhood isolated from healthy community.

The Cultural Gauge

We are products of our culture, even if our individualistic culture promises that we get to invent our "selves." In this century, the study of ecology has shown how deeply interconnected organisms are to one another and to their physical surroundings. Simultaneously, sociology has emerged as a social science, as humans begin to more fully understand the complexity of human society.

Each of us is born into a specific time, place, and culture. These cultures have significant shaping influences over our values, our sense of identity, and our purpose. In his book *The 3-D Gospel*, Jayson Georges distinguishes between guilt-innocence cultures, shame-honor cultures, and fear-power cultures. According to Georges, "a person's cultural orientation, or groupality, shapes their worldview, ethics, identity, and notion of salvation, even more than their individual personality does."[1] While Georges does not specifically mention decision-making, one's culture creates strong currents that affect one's approach to decisions.

While no culture is purely and simply one thing, these broad-stroke categories help to give language to different deeply shaping influences. It is quite possible to live in a nation mostly shaped by guilt-innocence culture while simultaneously growing up in a family with its own deeply embedded shame-honor culture. In this case, both would have competing influences in the decision-making process, adding complexity to an already complex decision. Let's look at each of these three cultural rubrics to see where they might be influencing our decisions—even when we aren't aware of them.

Guilt-innocence cultures are marked by strong notions of right and wrong and clear rules of acceptable and unacceptable behavior, sometimes spoken, sometimes unspoken. In these systems, moral responsibility becomes largely internalized since guilt needs no audience. The result is that constituents are encouraged to be largely autonomous, with slogans like "Think for yourself" and "Be true to yourself." Initially, this sounds like great freedom; however, the downside of such an autonomous, intuited approach to decision-making is crippling anxiety. Guilt-innocence cultures place a far heavier premium on career, hobby, and lifestyle choices than on family of origin or ethnicity. As such, decisions like career choice, neighborhood choice, and school choice become weightier than they need to be. If your individual choices define your deepest identity, already weighty decisions become even heavier. If you are not convinced, ask people graduating from college in America what they plan to do with their life. Their overwhelmed look will betray the weight of making decisions in a guilt-innocence culture.

Unlike guilt-innocence cultures, which place a high premium on the individual, honor-shame cultures focus on strong group orientations. If individual freedom is the currency of guilt-innocence cultures, obligation is the central currency of shame-honor cultures. People raised in these cultures see all of life through the lens of honor, which is defined as others thinking well of you and your family and which "creates harmonious social bonds in the community."[2] These cultures engender a deep fear of shame, which is "a negative public rating." In these cultures, decisions are primarily evaluated by asking, "Will this bring honor or shame to my family or group?"[3]

According to Georges, "Member of shame-honor cultures are expected to maintain the social status of the group, often at the expense of personal desires."[4] This creates obvious tensions when it comes to making decisions. For example, a student might feel torn between a career that is expected and revered within his or her culture and family and his or her internal passions and preferences. Similarly, someone within a shame-honor culture might feel shunned or shamed for choosing to marry someone outside of the expected culture or race.

In fear-power cultures, the focus tends to be more on unseen spiritual realms than on truths or ethical standards. In these cultures, "practices that placate the spiritual powers define acceptable human behavior."[5] Using dynamics of fear and power, leaders rely heavily on ritual practice to shape culture and behavior. While less common in Western culture, fear-power cultures have deep roots in Eastern and African cultures. They are also increasingly popular even in Western cultures that are pushing farther and farther away from Christian foundations and digging more deeply into ancient pagan beliefs and practices. Those shaped primarily in fear-power cultures tend to rely more heavily on signs, omens, and rituals when making decisions.

Each of these cultures has redemptive and fallen features, and no single culture has the corner on the market of biblical truth. For example, guilt-innocence cultures showcase the image of God in each individual while minimizing the communal nature of humanity. Conversely, shame-honor cultures show off the significance of community but can sometimes put the desire of the group in an idolatrous place. Fear-power cultures act as a check to the Western empire of empiricism in that they hold space for unseen powers and realities; however, they tend to limit the use of reason which was graciously gifted to humanity by our Creator.

By assessing which culture or combination of cultures has shaped you, you will be better able to understand the way it affects your approach to making decisions.

The Idolatry Gauge

Entire books have been dedicated to the concept of idolatry and the insidious ways that our hearts are idol-making factories. In ancient times, as God's people were being established, idolatry was obvious. Israel literally turned from their invisible God to visible idols crafted out of wood or metals (think of the golden calf moment at Mount Sinai), looking to created things rather than the Creator for security, significance, protection, and guidance. In our present cultural moment, idolatry has become much more sophisticated and insidious. Pastor Tim Keller has helped define an idol as "anything more important to you than God, anything that absorbs your heart and imagination more than God, anything you seek to give you what only God can give."[6]

At its heart, idolatry operates on inordinate desires or disordered affections. When a good thing becomes an ultimate thing, idolatry is at play. For example, the desire to have an ordered private world is a good desire when in its proper place; however, when the need to control becomes inordinate, it wreaks havoc in our homes and our hearts. Similarly, the desire for significance is a God-given human hunger meant to correlate with our significant role as the crown of God's creation (Ps. 8:5). We are hardwired for a significance that stems from our relationship with God; thus, when we attempt to seek significance through our careers, our body image, or our status, things go terribly awry.

It would be impossible to identify the controlling, out-of-order desires that direct and hijack every human heart, as our idolatry gauges are as unique as our experiences and stories. However, there are a few basic desires from which most of our idolatrous desires stem: love, security, success, power, and significance. If you want to discover the inordinate desires of your heart that direct your actions and choices, you can follow the trails made by your time, talents, and treasures. *To what does your mind wander when you wake up and before you go to bed? What are the fears that keep you up at night? Where do you spend most of your money? Where and for whom have you invested most of your time and energy? What or who, if taken away from you, would render your life seemingly hopeless or meaningless?*[7]

Whatever they may be, our idols have an oversized voice in our decision-making processes. If you idolize romantic love, you may rush prematurely into marriage. In your eagerness to count down the days until your wedding, you may not fully count the cost of the covenant you are making. If you idolize money, you may be tempted to take a promotion that does not fit your God-given gifting. If you idolize the approval of friends or bosses, you may find yourself saying things in the lunchroom or break room that you regret.

To make more reliable and God-honoring decisions, it is best to plumb the depths of our own hearts. Thankfully, we do not have to take these deep, cavernous dives alone. The third person of the Trinity peers where human eyes cannot see. As the apostle Paul told the Corinthian church, "The Spirit searches everything, even the depths of God" (1 Cor. 2:10). As you seek to identify the over-desires that direct the decisions you make, learn from the psalmist of old who prayed, "Search me, O God, and know my heart! Try me, and know my thoughts! And see if there be any grievous way in me, and lead me in the way everlasting" (Ps.139:23–24).

Once the inordinate desires of our hearts have been exposed, we are invited to repent and believe. There is no need for self-flagellation. The scarred hands of Jesus gently direct these good and right desires to himself, the place where they will find their perfect and ultimate satisfaction. Having been set in their proper places, these desires can become more trusted, right-sized gauges, providing helpful information as we seek to make decisions.

The Desire Gauge

In some cultures, universally agreed-upon societal or religious values undergird and direct decision-making, thereby eliminating many individual choices. Yet in our present culture, there are few such guides to keep decision-making in check. The individual self has become the monarch seeking to reign supreme, making decisions based almost entirely on pleasure and desire. While initially this sounds like freedom, it has created decision-making bondage in our generation. Self is crushed with the weight of decisions it was never intended to carry. In a vacuum of agreed-upon values and morals, individual desire often stands at the center of our decisions. As we discussed briefly in the first chapter, our age is dominated by the mantra "Follow your heart" and other such directives to do what feels right and good. However, the degree to which we feel a deep aversion to or desire for something does not determine whether it is right or wrong.

Pleasure and desire are not wrong in and of themselves; in fact, God is the one who dreamed up endorphins and dopamine, the neurotransmitters that give us pleasurable feelings. He is the ultimate artist who created a beautiful world full of colorful creations for his own pleasure as well as ours. Recent studies have shown we need emotion and intuition when making decisions. A neuroscientist named Antonio Damasio noticed a strange pattern in the decisions made by his patients who had experienced brain damage to the ventromedial part of the brain (the bottom-middle part of the brain behind the bridge of the nose that contributes to emotion). His patients, who still had the full ability to reason and use logic, were stumped and paralyzed by decisions, even small, seemingly simple ones. Because they were unable to access their emotions due to their injuries, their processes of decision-making were short-circuited.[8] Damasio's study flies in the face of the long-held ideas initiated by Plato that the ideal decision would be made by pure reason alone.

It seems God has wired the human brain to rely heavily upon emotion and desires while making decisions. As believers, this should not surprise us, as the Scriptures constantly show how God has knit humans together in body, mind, and soul. Just as historically some try to isolate reason and elevate it as the king of decision-making, others presently seek to isolate and elevate emotions as the ultimate decision decider. The Scriptures beautifully balance both. Our emotions and our reasoning are invited to have seats at the table, offering their distinct vantage points; however, for the Christian, Christ alone is king. Left unchecked, unexamined, and untrained by God and his word, desire and pleasure can become tyrants in the decision-making process with their tendency to overpromise and underdeliver.

In a world that makes decisions largely based on protecting personal freedom and receiving instant gratification, believers are invited to show off their set-apart nature as those who live with a deeper desire to honor and enjoy the Lord on an eternal timescale. The God who knit each of us uniquely in our mother's womb placed various pleasures, passions, and ambitions within us. As our preferences are trained increasingly by the word of God and focused on the one who is our deepest desire, they are invited to play a shaping role in our decision-making. While our inclinations alone are not determinative, they play directing roles in many of the decisions we make.

Hudson Taylor felt particularly called to China, while Amy Carmichael and Granny Brand were called to specific parts of India. They trusted God, who had placed these desires and burdens within them, to direct them, in part, through their sanctified desires. Teachers have passions that lead to preferences for which courses and grades they seek to teach. Accountants often feel God's pleasure creating and maintaining order in finances. When deciding between two equally wise college choices, prospective students rightly allow personal desires and preferences to impact their decision.

In his graciousness to us, God allows great freedom within the protective boundaries given through the Scriptures. As his word and his Spirit sanctify and straighten desires, they are invited to inform decisions big and small. We will explore the role of desire in our decisions further in chapter 6. For now, I mention the desire gauge to help you identify how much space it takes up on your specific dashboard of decisions.

The Urgency Gauge

As soon as we wake up in the morning, our hearts and minds are crowded with scores of thoughts, each demanding our full attention, each claiming to be urgent. Errands need to be run, monies need to be allocated, children need to be fed, and bills need to be paid. These loud demands labeled "Urgent" tend to steal our time and energies from the quiet things that are more important.

Using four quadrants (the urgent and important, the not urgent and important, the not important and urgent, and the not important and not urgent), Steven Covey helps to show the intersection between relative importance and urgency. In his observation and study, effective leaders spend most of their time and energy addressing decisions in the realm of the important and not urgent.[9] However, our lives and energies tend to be more strongly pulled by the urgency poles rather than the importance poles. It takes great effort and intentionality to spend our best mental and spiritual energies on the decisions that are most important, even when they do not feel urgent.

Charles Hummel wrote a short, power-packed pamphlet that brings a similar concept specifically into the life of a believer in Christ. Hummel writes what so many of us experience daily:

> We live in constant tension between the urgent and the important. The problem is that many important tasks need not be done today, or even this week. Extra hours of prayer and Bible study, a visit to an elderly friend, reading an important book: these activities can usually wait a while longer. But often urgent, though less important, tasks call for immediate response—endless demands pressure every waking hour.[10]

The tyranny of the urgent intersects with decision-making by laying far too much importance on a few major decision-making crossroads while rendering the daily and momentary crossroads insignificant. Major decisions like which school to attend, which major to declare, which job to pursue, and which house to purchase tend to have a monopoly on our time, thoughts, and energies.

While these major decisions are significant, the small decisions shape our habits, which, in turn, significantly shape our lives. The way we choose to spend our commute to work each day has as much, if not more, life-shaping power than the job we select. The way that we approach studying and learning has more of a lasting impact on our lives than the specific major written on our college diploma.

In his beautiful book *The Will of God as a Way of Life*, Jerry Sittser writes, "The most important decisions we make in life concern our way of life—habits, convictions, and direction."[11] In the Old Testament, the Hebrew word *derek*, meaning "course," "custom," or "way," occurs over seven hundred times. While occasionally it refers to an actual road, it often refers to the general direction, manner, and habits that make up one's life. In Psalm 32:8 the Lord writes through the psalmist, "I will instruct you and teach you in the way you should go; I will counsel you with my eye upon you." Here, the Lord is not promising a spiritual GPS system that will say "right" or "left" at the intersection of every major decision; rather, he is promising to instruct, teach, and counsel us in the habits and manners of our lives, helping us to be the kind of men and women who honor him in daily decisions.

Unfortunately, many of us have taken our cues from Hollywood, focusing most of our time and attention on large decision-making crossroads. We tend to pay little to no attention to the small decisions that direct the habits that powerfully direct our lives. We agonize over a handful of future decisions, all the while largely ignoring small opportunities to faithfully obey God in the present. We sit on the couch overthinking career decisions when we could be obeying God by serving our neighbor or sharing the gospel with a friend. As Sittser reminds us, "We can always do the will of God as we know it in the present moment, however confused we are about the future."[12]

In her writings, Elisabeth Elliot constantly stressed God's deep concern over the little things in our lives. Though she and her late husband Jim Elliot made huge decisions at critical times, the small, less urgent decisions they chose to make daily prepared them for the larger ones looming in the future:

> Has it ever happened with you that you have asked God to show you what He wants done about a certain matter, and His answer seems to be, "I am concerned now with something much smaller?" He sometimes shows me that the thing that looms large in importance to me is not nearly so important to God just now. He would rather I please him in some "minor" thing.[13]

Amid the urgent, God invites us to remember the important, not urgent, decisions we face daily. He who is faithful in the lesser can be entrusted with the greater (Luke 16:10). We should not despise the day of small things (Zech. 4:10). For it is often in the less urgent things that God does his most significant shaping work. The best preparation for the future is faithfully doing God's will today.[14]

The Gospel Gauge

For those who are in Christ, the gospel changes everything. The reality of Christ's life, death, and resurrection reconnects the God gauge at the center of the decision-making dashboard while simultaneously right-sizing the other gauges. In Christ, the needs of the human heart for significance, belonging, purpose, and security are met. As such, we no longer need to pander to the hungry needs of our hearts that are so accustomed to temporarily finding their rest through idols. These needs are sated in Christ who has eternally secured our place of approved standing before God. Christ provides the Comforter to give us a lasting security that does not depend upon circumstances. He frees us from the clamoring cacophony of our idols, which demand control, comfort, and significance. Put in their right place, these formerly controlling gauges can offer us insight without overly influencing our decisions.

As someone who grew up in the upper-middle class in America, I was deeply influenced by the desire to achieve significance through academic performance. I loved learning and came by it naturally; thus, my family assumed that I should be a doctor. After all, doctors hold a prestigious, money-making role in our culture. I threw myself into an unrivaled pursuit of excellence, oblivious to the fact that my significance and security gauges were playing an exaggerated role in my decision-making processes. In college, as my gospel gauge grew in centrality and preeminence, my security and significance gauges shrank accordingly. I switched between a biology major, a tried-and-true path to medicine, and an English major, the place of my passions, a record number of times. My heart was torn between what I thought I should do and what I desperately wanted to do. My cultural hardwiring conflicted with the rewiring the gospel was doing in my life. I kept switching dashboards until I was dizzied; eventually, I lived in limbo by choosing to double major.

Looking back, I can so clearly see how my gauges were off. My approval gauge relied far too heavily on what my professors and parents expected and hoped for me. My security gauge did not account for the fact that God provides for his children in ways that do not make sense in a monetarily minded culture. I had a shrunken, almost nonexistent desire gauge. It would take years until I found the lanes where I sensed God's pleasure and my passions meeting. Yet God, in his providence and faithfulness, directed my footsteps into the path that would give him the most glory and make me most like him. My biology degree is gathering dust, while I am actively using my English degree for God's glory and the good of the body of Christ.

My dear friend who is studying to be a pilot spends countless hours in the cockpit during training flights, check rides, and simulations. He assures me that the more often we learn to check our gauges, the more natural the process will become. In time, like pilots who synthesize complex information from a quick glance at their dashes, we will become increasingly adept at understanding the input that informs our decisions. It may be overwhelming at first, but an honest assessment of our decision-making dashboards will greatly help us as we wrestle with the decisions set before us.

5

Practical Preparation
for Decisions

MY HUSBAND AND I BOTH spend our lives in the unfinished work of vocational ministry. While we love our callings to spiritual formation, we tend to find ourselves drawn to household projects on the weekends. In the messy, ever-incomplete work of ministry, there is something deeply satisfying about completing a to-do list. My husband does woodworking projects while I stick to painting projects.

Anyone who has painted a room knows the preparation for painting, while tedious, is just as significant as the painting itself. In fact, when the preparation is complete, the actual work of painting becomes far more efficient. A few hours of removing furniture, unscrewing electrical plates, and applying painter's tape makes the hours of painting much more effective. In the same way, taking the appropriate time and energy to prepare for the decisions we make enables the process to be less frustrating and far more freeing. Setting proper expectations, gathering the proper pieces of information, and inviting others into our decisions free us to experience less headache and heartache and more joy.

Proper Expectations

Healthy expectations free us from some unnecessary frustration when making decisions. Had Gilligan and crew known that they were in for more than a three-hour tour, they could have packed and prepared differently. We don't have to be caught off guard by the complexity and ambiguity of the decision-making process. The more realistic we are in our expectations, the better!

Clarity

Author Brennan Manning recounts a powerful story about an ethicist named John Kavanaugh. Like many searching for a clear sense of calling, Kavanaugh found himself traveling to Calcutta in search of direction from Mother Teresa. When she asked him what he needed from her, he asked her to pray for clarity, only to have Mother Teresa flat out refuse his request. Bewildered, Kavanaugh retorted "that *she* always seemed to have the clarity he longed for," to which Mother Teresa laughed and said, "I have never had clarity; what I have always had is trust. So I will pray that you trust God."[1]

We far too easily demand clarity from our Creator when, instead of clarity, he would rather cultivate faith in us. Obviously, clarity remains an end goal of the process of decision-making; however, faith precedes clarity. The writer of Hebrews reminds us that faith is "the assurance of things hoped for, the conviction of things not seen" (Heb. 11:1). Later in the same chapter, he also reminds us that "without faith it is impossible to please [God]" (Heb. 11:6). Every decision, even those well-thought-out and prayed through, requires faith of some sort. It takes faith to stay in the states to minister in our neighborhoods just as it requires faith to leave the states to share the gospel in a foreign context. It takes faith to walk as a single man or woman just as it takes faith to enter the covenant of marriage with a spouse. It takes faith to foster children not knowing how long they may be with you, but it also takes faith to say a prayerful no to a potential foster placement.

Thus, when we are asking the Lord to give ample clarity, it is helpful to recognize that even decisions that have become clear require trusting faith.

Complexity

Sometimes decisions are short, sweet, and simple. There is no need to agonize over which sides to select with your entree at a restaurant, though some of us do struggle between the steamed veggies and the side salad. When choices revolve around neutral, amoral, personal preferences, the consequences of the decision are rarely weighty. However, when decisions involve the more significant pieces of our lives, the process becomes increasingly complex.

Many of the decisions that cause the most agony in life are not decisions between good and bad but rather those that require us to discern the ever-thin lines between good, better, and best. Sometimes "moral convictions can collide and compete."[2] If we have competing values that are all biblical, the decision-making process becomes increasingly complex. For example, as parents we place a high value on our physical children and also on the spiritual children God has entrusted to us through the college ministry we serve. Since both are biblically good, they feel like competitors for our evenings and our attention. Rather than creating an absolute rule, we approach each week differently, asking God for wisdom as we plan our schedules.

In Romans 12:1–2 the apostle Paul instructs believers regarding how to discern God's will. He appeals to them, considering who they are in Christ, to offer their bodies as living sacrifices, which initially sounds like an oxymoron. After all, in the cultural context in which Paul was writing, the word *sacrifice* conjured images of bloody animals on altars. However, in light of Christ's once-for-all, completely sufficient sacrifice of himself upon the cross (Heb. 10:4) Paul reframes Christian worship, inviting believers to make choices that are "holy and acceptable to God." He writes, "Do not be conformed to this world, but be transformed by the renewal of your mind, that by testing you may discern what is the will of God, what is good and acceptable and perfect" (Rom. 12:2).

Paul focuses more on the formation of our souls than on offering a formula for decision-making. The world constantly shapes us through advertising and media, even when we are not aware of its shaping power. In order to have our minds constantly realigned, we need regular, steady intake of God's word with God's people.

To counteract the hours in which we are being actively or passively shaped by the world around us, weekly worship within the local church stands paramount. While it may not always feel earth-shattering or eternally shaping, regularly sitting under God's word as it's taught to God's people shapes us as waves shape the jagged rocks of jetties. Rarely does a wave hit a rock in such a way as to rip off an entire jagged edge. Rather, the regular washing by the daily tides slowly rounds and shapes the rocks over years.

The same stands true for daily time in God's word. While we may favor five more minutes of sleep or one more episode of the show we recently discovered, even short segments of time personally spent reading and studying the Scriptures powerfully shape us. While looking up a handful of verses that relate to the decision at hand is helpful, it can never substitute for an ongoing intake of God's life-changing word. Just as vitamins are meant to supplement healthy eating habits, entrenched habits of devotion posture us to make wise decisions.

When our minds are being shaped and reshaped primarily by the word of God, we are prepared to take part in decision-making as another avenue of worship to God. We will have the sharpness of soul and sight that can help delineate between good, better, and best.

Only when our minds are more shaped by God and his values than by the surrounding world can we have the clarity of thought to discern the will of God moment by moment, decision by decision.

Christ, the Pioneer

When we face an important or especially befuddling decision, we naturally seek out those who have made a similar decision before us. A family I know interviewed a handful of missionary families before deciding to uproot their lives in obedience to God's call to a country halfway around the world. Before deciding to apply to law school, it is natural to meet with others who themselves considered the same course of action. In doing such research and networking relationships, we seek a pattern and a pioneer. While these are, indeed, helpful, our souls will be most served by looking to Christ, the ultimate pioneer.

He knows the end from the beginning (Isa. 46:10). The reality that Christ stands outside of time, sovereignly steering not only human history but also our lives, anchors us in the choppy waters of complex decisions. God already knows all our days, which he has carefully written (Ps. 139:16). In Christ we have a pioneer who has gone ahead of us and before us, as the writer of Hebrews so powerfully explains in Hebrews 12:2. Christ, the founder and perfecter of our faith, is both prior and pioneer. When we face the decisions that can sometimes cripple, it calms our hearts to remember that we have one who has gone before, who hems us in behind and before (Ps. 139:5–6). Amid all the unknowns, we know the one who walks beside us, the one who lives within us, and the one who has gone ahead of us. We may not know the map, but we know the character of our guide.

Now that we have healthy expectations on the decision-making process, we can begin gathering the pieces necessary to solve the puzzling decisions before us.

Gathering the Pieces

Upon graduating from college, I found myself unexpectedly teaching biology at a small high school. I entered the world of classroom management with blind spots and no training as an educator. I looked like a deer in headlights for most of the year, as I learned how to write lesson plans, manage behavior, and input grades in real time.

In his graciousness to me, the Lord provided an unexpected mentor and life coach in the form of an adjunct anatomy teacher, Dr. Wines. After having taught anatomy and physiology at a prestigious university, he left academia to pursue full-time vocational ministry. As he attended seminary, he taught advanced-placement courses at our little Christian school. Those students had no idea the gift that they had received in him, but the gift was not lost on me.

Dr. Wines would often find me overwhelmed in the teachers' lounge, locked in battle with my nemesis, the copy machine. As he coached me through my copier trouble, he would also counsel me about calling and vocation. He was the first to teach me that decision-making is often like doing a puzzle. When one opens a new jigsaw puzzle, the best thing to do is lay out all the pieces, right-side up, on the table. He reminded me that, regarding decisions, our job is to look for the pieces God offers us throughout our days, weeks, months, and years. The hard work is gathering the pertinent pieces. Once we have done our part in collecting a crucial number of them, the picture on the puzzle begins to take shape.

Periodically, Dr. Wines would ask me what I had learned about myself in the previous few weeks. His piercing questions helped illuminate the little pieces of information that I might have otherwise overlooked as I trudged through my first year of teaching. Bit by bit, Dr. Wines helped me to see that while I did not love classroom management or teaching the Krebs Cycle, I came alive teaching the Scriptures and theology. His encouragement to look for little pieces of critical information enabled me to begin to unlock the puzzle of my vocation.

As much as we may want the piece-gathering stage to happen quickly and on our own timetables, often, the pieces are provided slowly as we experience daily life. In fact, we tend to miss many of the opportunities to gather pieces because they are hidden in the monotony of mundane living. Probing questions asked during intentionally planned moments of rest and reflection help us to identify potential pieces that could make the puzzle come together.

Zola Neale Hurston wisely wrote, "There are years that ask questions and years that answer them."[3] When we are in a year (or a month or week) that asks questions, we may be tempted to rush the process to get to answers. However, God invites us to wait with him and for him. Isaiah 64:4 powerfully reminds us, "From of old no one has heard or perceived by the ear, no eye has seen a God besides you, who acts for those who wait for him." While we wait, we are invited to have our eyes open and expectantly lifted to God while also gathering the little bits of wisdom and insight he scatters into our waiting.

Pivotal Pieces

When it comes to decision-making, the puzzles are as nuanced and unique as the people seeking to put them together. However, a few common pivotal pieces of information aid in the decision-making process. Taking the time to gather critical pieces regarding our passions, our priorities, and our providential circumstances will serve us well as we seek to make decisions.

Passions

The same God who delights to make snowflakes, no two of which are alike, has created an incredibly diverse humanity. As plentiful personality tests and assessments prove, humans are hardwired with different personalities, passions, talent pools, and tendencies. While personality tests can be taken too far and can sometimes encourage our sinful predisposition to self-obsession, they do provide helpful landing points for self-discovery.

In his *Institutes*, John Calvin speaks of double knowledge, saying, "Nearly all wisdom we possess, that is to say, true and sound wisdom, consists of two parts: the knowledge of God and of ourselves."[4] These two knowledges ought to rightly feed into and shape the other. True knowledge of self comes from true knowledge of God, and true knowledge of God will lead to a right view of self. If it is our deep desire to experience what Jesus spoke about in John 10 as life to the fullest, we would do well to be lifelong learners of self. Far from being self-obsessed, true knowledge of self, which will include an honest assessment of spiritual and natural gifting as well as limitations and weaknesses, will press us further into humble worship of the God who made us.

In addition to spiritual gift assessments, common grace assessments (Myers-Briggs, CliftonStrengths, RightPath, etc.) can provide helpful insight into the way both our nature and our nurture have shaped us.

One of our dear friends used to serve in campus ministry in a student-facing role that was filled with one-on-one conversations, lunches, and dinners. Although she fully believed in the mission of her organization, she found herself exhausted and frustrated at the end of each day. After a year of faithfully struggling, my husband and I sat down to evaluate with her. As we all came to find out, our dear friend was better wired for complex tasks and behind-the-scenes leadership. In fact, years earlier, when she was an elementary-aged girl, our friend had literally asked for a filing cabinet for Christmas! The facts were all right in front us, but it took time to put all the pieces of her passion and gifting together. After switching her to an office role, our friend excelled to the point of eventually leading a large team for a larger organization.

Priorities

Passions alone do not dictate our decisions. In addition to assessing our unique passions, we are invited to evaluate our priorities, which often change depending on age, stage, and season of life. Unlike the world, which tells us that we can do everything and have everything, the Scriptures remind us that we are derivative creatures with built-in limitations (Ps. 90:12). Rather than hinder us, the limitations on our time, energy, and focus can help us. They force us to focus on a few priorities, allowing us to intentionally accomplish the good works that the Lord has prepared in advance for us to walk in (Eph. 2:10).

A dear friend of mine is finishing her seminary degree, as she has a passion to see women equipped to study and teach the word of God. While she knows that a ministry role is likely in her future, her present priorities have her focused at home as the mother of a newborn and a toddler. However, in subsequent seasons her priorities will shift, allowing her more time and bandwidth to pursue her desire in a more focused way.

Questions help us to evaluate our priorities. Quarterly, my husband and I pull away from the busyness of life to evaluate, reevaluate, and realign our priorities and our lives. We ask and fight to answer questions like, "What is there that only I can do in this season?" and, "What are the critical roles in our lives in this season?" (e.g., child of God, son, parent, employee, deacon). Next, we come up with a few goals for each of our roles. These questions have helped to direct us through multiple decisions as a couple and a family. For example, although I absolutely loved my role as women's ministry director at our church, I chose to step down to create more space and availability for my marriage and our teenage sons who will be navigating a very crucial season of life. I hope to pick up official women's ministry again in the future, but the knowledge of my priorities has freed me to make a difficult decision in full confidence.

Providential Circumstances

In addition to assessing our passions and priorities, it is helpful to assess the present providential circumstances in which the Lord has placed us. In Psalm 16 David paints a beautiful picture of the Lord as one lovingly and sovereignly assigning the circumstances and lots of his particular people:

> The LORD is my chosen portion and my cup;
>> you hold my lot.
> The lines have fallen for me in pleasant places;
>> indeed, I have a beautiful inheritance.
>
> I bless the LORD who gives me counsel;
>> in the night also my heart instructs me.
> I have set the LORD always before me;
>> because he is at my right hand, I shall not be shaken.
>> (Ps. 16:5–8)

While the poem sounds lovely, we should be careful to remember that the underlying principle did not always feel lovely to David. While David experienced beautiful seasons of comfortable circumstances, he also walked through challenging circumstances. Whether he was running for his life from the jealous Saul or being betrayed by his own son, David believed that a sovereign God allowed every situation and circumstance in his life. As such, he sought the Lord for wisdom and counsel as he made decisions daily.

An honest assessment of the present circumstances that the Lord has drawn up for each of us may help direct our decision-making processes. For example, I have a dear friend who has been out of work for a prolonged season. Though she is a brilliant research scientist who is well-qualified for the scores of jobs for which she has applied, doors have continually shut. While she was initially devastated and confused by these circumstances, she has slowly begun to see that God might be using her long unemployment to redirect her toward a different lane in the same scientific highway. Her years of cancer research have intersected with a friend's terminal cancer diagnosis, and she has found herself helping him navigate through potential trials and treatments. These providential circumstances have helped to direct her to make the decision to begin a new career as a cancer patient advocate. She is now seeking to use her expertise to bless families overwhelmed by cancer diagnoses by helping explain their options in a down-to-earth and personal way.

In his memoir, Pastor Stuart Briscoe recalled wise advice he received as he faced a considerable life decision. As a successful banker who saw the marketplace as the mission field it was, he felt torn between continuing in it or committing himself to full-time ministry. His mentor shared simple advice that served him and will serve us as well: "Stuart, push plenty of doors; don't try to knock any down."[5] In this witty way, his mentor urged him to look at the present circumstances around him. Briscoe rightly reasoned, "If God has a plan for our lives, he would be more interested in us finding it than we could ever be."

By exploring open doors, Briscoe was able to actively assess what God might be communicating through the opportunities presenting themselves around him. While every need is not a call, God does often use the setting and scenes of our lives to help direct us. In his case, doors continued to open for both paths. Thus, he had to make the difficult decision. He spent time gathering the necessary pieces of information about himself, his present circumstances, and his priorities. Although two paths were opening before him and his wife, they could pursue only one. At the end of the day, the Briscoes' priority of wanting to train up the next generation led them to quit a lucrative job at the bank to help train lay leaders at Capernwray Bible School.

I wish gathering the pieces for significant decisions were as simple as overturning a prepackaged jigsaw puzzle box. However, gathering the pieces often feels like searching in a scavenger hunt. As we discussed in chapter 2, the process of decision-making is often as significant as the decision that is made. We need eyes outside of our own to help identify our passions, priorities, and providential circumstances.

Blind Spots

Two years ago our family purchased a car with some features we have never had before. While my children love the seat warmers, I am most thankful for its blind-spot detection system. On busy

California highways and interchanges, the blinking orange light on the rearview mirrors makes driving much less stressful. If only there was similar technology for helping us identify the blind spots in our decision-making.

While our culture would lead us to believe we are self-sufficient, humans are, by nature, limited creatures. We were created for interdependence. We need others to gently point out blind spots and biases. As Jane Austen so succinctly wrote, "How quick come the reasons for approving what we like!"[6] Our hearts are quick to justify our own views and preferences. In order to get a more holistic view, it is helpful to invite others to share their perspectives and vantage points.

Solomon offered similar wisdom in the book of Proverbs: "Without counsel plans fail, but with many advisors they succeed" (Prov. 15:22). While inviting a few trusted people to speak into our decisions does not guarantee that they will be successful, wisdom bids us seek the counsel of those who know both the word of God and our specific situations well. I like to call these carefully chosen counselors "trusted trespassers."

Trusted Trespassers

We all have hiding places we would rather others not find. As complex humans we can build elaborate walls and defenses. We also tend to have selective hearing, often listening only to those who tell us what we want to hear. In "Mending Wall," Robert Frost wrote about walls and fences:

> Before I built a wall I'd ask to know
> What I was walling in or walling out,

And to whom I was like to give offense.
Something there is that doesn't love a wall,
That wants it down.

Humans build elaborate walls and defenses, but simultaneously long to be known. We put up "No Trespassing" signs, all the while looking to be known. Trusted trespassers are a select few who will love us enough to ignore our "No Trespassing" signs, ask hard questions, and offer truths we may not want to hear. As Proverbs 27:6 warns us, "Faithful are the wounds of a friend; profuse are the kisses of an enemy."

Trusted trespassers should be fluent in the gospel. They are easy to identify because their lives are stained by the Scriptures. Through years of experience, they have learned how to apply the word of God to daily life. The more these trespassers know about you and your circumstances, the better. Unfortunately, it is all too easy to surround ourselves with people who tell us what we want to hear rather than people who tell us what we need to hear. When choosing your trusted trespassers, try to select people of different generations and experiences.

When seeking counsel from trusted trespassers, also be careful to make your aim to please God, not man. As Paul rhetorically asked the Galatian church, we are invited to regularly check our hearts by asking, "Am I now seeking the approval of man, or of God?" (Gal. 1:10). There may be times when God is calling us to do something that may go against the advice of a trusted friend. In such moments, our decisions should be bathed in prayer and founded on the word of God rather than the opinions of men.

After Elisabeth Elliot's husband was brutally murdered by some of the men he was trying to reach, she faced an incredibly difficult decision. Would she continue the work that she and her husband had begun? As a widowed mother of a young daughter, her parents and trusted friends all questioned her desire to return to the Auca people; however, Elisabeth saw an opportunity to tangibly show God's forgiveness to the people who had left her widowed. She saw the conflicting advice of her friends and family as the Lord's means to test the validity of her call. If everyone else told her it was unwise, but she was certain the Lord was bidding her to bring the gospel to the Auca, to whom would she listen? She said, "My awareness of God's will for me, far from making me deaf to godly advice, made me listen the more carefully and wait with greater patience and quietness for the final signal."[7] When providential circumstances opened a way for her to head back to the Auca, she knew it was time to walk in fearful faith!

When we invite the voices of godly counsel to the table of our decisions, we should fight to listen to the word of God and the Spirit's guidance through it.

Learning to Listen

Listening to God through his word and prayer in the moments of mundane days postures us to be able to listen to him in the momentous crossroads of major decisions. The prophet Isaiah speaks of his own habitual posture of listening to the Lord, proclaiming, "Morning by morning he awakens; he awakens my ear to hear as those who are taught. The Lord GOD has opened my ear, and I was not rebellious; I turned not backward" (Isa. 50:4–5).

Elisabeth Elliot counseled women seeking guidance to cultivate habits of faithful listening to the Lord through the Scriptures. She reminded them that God may not give all the required pieces for the decision at one time but rather bit by bit and day by day:

> Guidance for a decision that need not be final until next Wednesday may require one small move or commitment today. I accept that and act on it without haggling with God because he has not granted me all the information I'm itching for. . . . I may rest in his love, confident that when the time is ripe, the guidance will be clear.[8]

Similarly, Jesus himself spoke to his disciples about their need to be accustomed to his voice. Using the powerful and culturally accessible language of shepherding, Jesus told his friends, "The sheep hear his voice, and he calls his own sheep by name and leads them out" (John 10:3). He elaborated upon the intimacy and regularity of the relationship between the sheep and shepherd, saying, "The sheep follow him, for they know his voice" (John 10:4). Jesus states the sheep are so familiar with the voice of their shepherd that "a stranger they will not follow, but they will flee from him, for they do not know the voice of strangers" (John 10:5).

While images of sheep with shepherds may seem the stuff of baby nurseries or farm movies to our modern ears, the disciples would have heard great warmth and wisdom in Jesus's chosen imagery. Phillip Keller, a shepherd by trade, wrote fondly of the hours and years spent with his flocks, huddled in caves for protection from the cold, leading them away from dangerous herbs that would hurt their digestive systems to healthy pasture.

He knew their personalities so intimately that he had nicknames for each of them. He led his flock daily, sometimes with poking and prodding.[9]

The sheep knew Keller's voice. They listened to him when he cajoled them to follow him toward fresh water and new pastures so they would not overgraze to their own detriment. Similarly, we are invited to become well-acquainted with our good shepherd's voice. If we cultivate habits of listening to him in the mundane decisions of daily life, we will be better able to discern his voice in the major decisions.

Through cultivating habits of daily devotional time with God in his word, weekly times of extended solitude and silence, and quarterly evaluation of our walk with God, we grow in familiarity with the voice of our shepherd. We begin to know not only the words he speaks but also his diction and tone. The more we know his voice, the less likely we will be fooled by impostors and lesser lovers who might seek to lead us in a different direction.

Staying close to the shepherd and straining to hear his voice will enable Christ to gently lead us. It is much better to follow him daily from devotion than to be forcefully but faithfully goaded. David, who had seasons in which he experienced both, wrote, "Be not like a horse or a mule, without understanding, which must be curbed with bit and bridle, or it will not stay near you" (Ps. 32:9). Our faithful God will keep and direct his people; however, the way we posture ourselves toward him will affect our experience of that direction. May we not be stubborn like the Old Testament prophet Balaam. Because he did not listen to God's subtle leading, God graciously opened the mouth of his donkey to stop him from going further (Num. 22:22–35). While this type of intervention was miraculous, it was also incredibly indicting of Balaam's inability to listen to God's guidance leading up to that moment.

A Word of Warning

When speaking about listening to God, it's helpful to understand how God speaks. The writer of Hebrews reminds Jewish believers that Christ is God's ultimate and final word. Though he used to speak through prophets, "in these last days he has spoken to us by his Son, whom he appointed the heir of all things, through whom also he created the world" (Heb. 1:1–2).

Christ is God's best and final word to us. The entire canon of the Scriptures points to him. On the road to Emmaus, Jesus taught two distraught disciples how all the Scriptures point to him (Luke 24:27). While many seek an individual, nuanced word from God himself, the old hymn *How Firm a Foundation* points us to God's final word:

> How firm a foundation, ye saints of the Lord,
> is laid for your faith in His excellent Word!
> What more can He say than to you He hath said,
> who unto the Savior for refuge have fled?

In his own final words to his protégé, Timothy, the apostle Paul charges Timothy to live his entire life under the whole counsel of God. He reminds Timothy that "all Scripture is breathed out by God and profitable" to the end that the "man of God may be complete, equipped for every good work" (2 Tim. 3:16–17). In making decisions and seeking to listen to the good shepherd, we can be comforted to know that he speaks through the Scriptures.

The Holy Spirit will never lead us to do something against the God-breathed words he inspired through the various writers. While the principles of Scripture require that Spirit-led and nuanced wisdom be applied to our lives and situations, God will never guide his people away from the words he has so graciously provided for us!

Preparation and Prayer

In this chapter we have sought to establish healthy expectations regarding the decision-making process (clarity, complexity, and Christ as pioneer). We've identified some pivotal pieces to the puzzle (passions, priorities, and providential circumstances). We've underscored the need for trusted trespassers who will help point out blind spots while pointing us to Jesus. In a chapter devoted to practical preparation, there is one final practice left to address: the practice of prayer.

Prayer is to the soul what breath is to the body. Even Jesus himself had a custom of rising early in the morning to connect and converse with his Father (Mark 1:35). In addition to the constant ongoing prayer conversation Jesus kept with his Father, he sometimes spent prolonged times praying, often before significant decisions. Before he selected his twelve disciples, Jesus pulled an all-nighter praying to the Father (Luke 6:12). When he was in the throes of the most significant decision of his life, he spent hours agonizing in prayer in the garden of Gethsemane (Matt. 26:36–46; Mark 14:32–42; Luke 22:39–46). If Jesus himself relied upon the practice of prayer, how much more should we!

In prayer, we pour out our hearts and lives in utter dependence upon God (Ps. 62:8). We invite him into our hearts to search our motivations (Ps. 139:23–24). We beg for him to send out his light and truth to lead us to more of him (Pss. 43:3–4; 119:125). Prayer brings us into the presence of God, allowing the decisions and dilemmas that have our attention to be set within the backdrop of God's greater story.

When it comes to prayer and decision-making, we may be tempted to bring our own plans to the Lord merely for his stamp of approval. Sometimes we subtly use prayer as an attempt to bend God's will toward our preference. However, prayer does quite the opposite. It makes our hearts malleable and bends our wills to his (Isa. 29:6; 64:8).

In addition to our individual prayer lives, God's word invites us to pray with others (James 5:13–16). Just as the early church often gathered to seek the Lord's wisdom in confusing or complex situations, we are encouraged to pray with others over the decisions that keep us up at night (Acts 2:42–44; 12:1–5). Even the apostle Paul, who had a thriving personal prayer life, invited the church to pray for specific decisions and needs (Col. 4:2–4). It has often been my experience that God provides clarity and valuable insight when two or three are gathered to pray (Matt.18:20).

Fasting

Intricately linked to the practice of prayer is the spiritual discipline of fasting. We live in a culture of indulgence and plenty in which we often have far more than we need to eat, wear, and do. In such a culture, the idea of fasting can sound archaic, ascetic, and unnecessary. However, because we *do* live in such a culture, fasting is a discipline that may help us far more than we could ever imagine.

Fasting refers to abstaining from food for spiritual purposes, but often the principles underneath food fasting can be applied to other arenas of our lives: shopping, technology, Netflix, coffee, and the like (Matt. 9:15). Richard Foster captures the purpose for fasting:

> Fasting reminds us that we are sustained "by every word that proceeds from the mouth of God" (Matthew 4:4). Food does not sustain us; God sustains us. In Christ, "All things hold together" (Colossians 1:17). Therefore, in experiences of fasting we are not so much abstaining on food as we are feasting on the word of God. Fasting is feasting.[10]

Specifically, when facing a difficult decision, fasting exposes the fears and driving motivations of our hearts. Nehemiah, Jehoshaphat, Daniel, and countless biblical figures fasted in order to focus on seeking the Lord's will before difficult decisions. As we fast, our physical hunger underscores our spiritual hunger. Fresh reminders of our physical limitations help to highlight our desperate need for wisdom from God.

Prayer and fasting pair well together to prime our hearts to hear from the Lord. In our haste to want to act and move forward with making decisions, we sometimes neglect these two disciplines; however, no one will ever regret taking time to spiritually prepare his or her heart. Moments or hours spent lingering in the presence of the Lord is time well spent.

6

Practical Paradigms for Decisions

WHILE MY TWO SISTERS AND I were growing up, our late grandmother invited us to travel the world with her. I wish you could have known her, as she was four feet eleven inches of sass and silliness. One summer, we traveled to the Grecian Islands. Outside of my grandmother repeatedly calling the currency "dracula" instead of "drachma," we loved Greece. Out of all the islands we visited, Santorini was by far our favorite.

If you have ever seen pictures of white clay houses with bright blue–domed ceilings nestled on cliffs, you were looking at Santorini. The horseshoe-shaped island is the caldera that remained after a volcano erupted. Clay switchback trails lead up steep embankments from the bay to the village that sits at the top. The quaint village is nestled atop the steep walls. On the other side of the picturesque houses, the island boasts rare black beaches. We had only six hours to cover the terrain, but I wish we could have stayed for six weeks. Though I experienced Santorini in parts and pieces, the island itself is a unified whole. The steep embankments were caused by the same volcano that blackened the beaches, though they were separated by substantial amounts of space. As a human being living within the limitations of time and space, I cannot experience and see all of Santorini at once. I stand in various places at separate times experiencing different perspectives.

I share this story, not only to encourage you to put Santorini on top of your travel wish list, but also to introduce the very significant topic of perspective. Theologian and professor John Frame defines *perspective* simply as "a position from which a person sees something."[1] Frame explains: "a person's perspective is the standpoint from which he gains his overall understanding of the world."[2] Defined as such, we need to take a longer look at the perspectives from which we, as decision makers, approach not only the decision at hand but also the world at large.

An Introduction to Triperspectivalism

Unlike humans who are limited in perspective, our God is omniscient, which is to say that he knows all things. However, Frame points out that not only does God know all things, but he also "sees all things from every possible perspective," which means that "God is not only omniscient but omniperspectival."[3] Using Santorini as an example, God not only knows Santorini as it was in the past as an active volcano, but he also sees it in its present state as a thin crescent-shaped caldera. Being outside of time, he also knows how it will look in five hundred years. Similarly, he can know every part of Santorini from every possible perspective. He sees it from the eyes of a hawk soaring above, a starfish living on its craggy shores, and the woeful donkey carrying the heavy load of tourism up its embankments.

Frame uses triperspectivalism as a teaching tool by which believers can approach the complexity of God's word and his world. Recognizing the ubiquitous nature of triads in the Scriptures, seen most significantly through the triune nature of God, Frame builds triperspectivalism to approach complex truths from different angles and perspectives. Frame condenses the unique attributes of each person of the Trinity into three lordship attributes: authority, control, and presence. These lordship attributes lead three distinct perspectives or lenses to approach the word and the world: the normative, the situational, and the existential.

God's authority, which correlates most strongly to the action and attributes of God the Father, can be summed up in the word *normative*. When we think of the normative perspective, "we learn of God as the lawgiver, the one who legislates our conduct, the one who rewards and punishes our behavior."[4] God's control, which correlates most strongly to the action and attributes of Jesus the Son, can be summed up in the world *situational*. When we think of the situational, we think of Christ's control of circumstances and situations, the history of God's people, and the work that Jesus has done to redeem us. God's presence correlates to the action and attributes of God the Holy Spirit and can be summed up in the word *existential*. When we think of the existential, we think of the Spirit's internal work of renewal through regeneration and sanctification and his intimate nearness to believers as the indwelling presence of God.

Remember, all of God does all that God does, so these three different perspectives bleed into and feed into one another; however, the three-perspective approach gives us different entry points into the nature of God's word and his world. Just as a huge cathedral may have multiple entry points that provide different perspectives on the one unified building, the normative, the situational, and the existential provide different doors into the Godhead and different lenses by which to view our decisions (among many other things).

We are limited people looking at the world, our lives, and our decisions from time- and space-bound perspectives. As such, Frame's framework (pun intended) gives us language and scaffolding that will enable us to look at the decisions at hand from all angles and perspectives.

Three Perspectives on Decision-Making

When we begin the decision-making process from the normative perspective, we are primarily asking the question, "What has God clearly said about this topic or decision in his word?" We comb the Scriptures for themes and principles that might inform the decision at hand. Take for example, marriage, one of the most significant decisions many people make in their lifetimes. If you are seriously dating someone and wrestling through the potential of marrying, you must investigate what God's word has to say about marriage. The normative perspective on marriage would narrow Christian marriage to a man and a woman. God created a gendered creation and officiated the first marriage in the first two chapters of Genesis, which makes marriage a creation ordinance. Paul's warning about becoming unequally yoked with an unbeliever in 2 Corinthians 6:14 would offer further wisdom on the subject. Ephesians 5 would provide a broad-stroke picture of the purpose of marriage as being for our holiness and not merely our happiness.

Now, let's approach the marriage question from the situational perspective, which would ask questions about the present circumstances of the lives of the two people at hand. For the sake of the example, let's imagine that our couple met in college while serving in the same Christian ministry (which makes the normative questions moot, as they share the same passions, training, experiences, and biblical convictions). From the situational perspective, they find themselves both graduating from college and planning to join the workforce in the United States. They plan to live on the same continent and are willing to settle in the same city. Their families and friends who have spent time with them affirm them as a couple and have seen them as healthy complements to one another. Thus, from a situational perspective, there are no major red flags or obstacles to overcome.

Finally, let's attempt to approach the same question from the existential perspective, which asks more internal questions about personal desires, feelings, and passions. Even though our imaginary couple has moved through the normative and situational perspectives easily, they are invited to ask the existential questions. From this perspective, they will seek to sift through their layered desires. They will seek to determine if they are simply excited about the idea of marriage or are truly excited about each other. Is this the person that each wants to walk through life's peaks and valleys alongside?

For the sake of practice, let's press another common yet crucial decision through the triperspectival paradigm. My husband and I have watched countless believers graduate from college and begin to navigate critical decisions regarding the local church. As such, we are more convinced than ever that church membership remains one of the most shaping decisions a believer can make. When coaching graduates and friends through this deeply significant decision, we often take a triperspectival approach.

Beginning with the normative, we ask the significant questions of theology, ecclesiology, and eschatology: Does this church preach the Scriptures exegetically? Does it take a Christ-centered approach to the Scriptures? What are the beliefs of the denomination? What is the church's polity?

Then we seek to look at the decision from a situational approach: How far is the church from where you are planning to live? Do you have other trusted friends and family who also attend this church? Is the spiritual formation strategy of the church accessible and feasible for you in this season of life?

Finally, we would help the would-be decision maker approach the question from the final existential perspective: What type of church did you grow up in? In what ways has that shaped you into who you are and are becoming? When you attend this church, are you ushered into the presence of God? Would you seek to emulate the elders and leaders of this church? What are the most critical needs in your spiritual development? Does this church offer teaching, training, and encouragement in that area?

While triperspectivalism does not answer the question at hand, it does provide a manageable, multifaceted way to approach a decision. I often liken the decision-making process to untying a complex knot. Initially, the process can seem utterly overwhelming if we do not have an entry point and a method to slowly tease apart different strands of the knot. At first our fingers seem clumsy and uncoordinated, but with practice and patience, loop by loop, we learn to tease out the truth with the help of the Spirit of God, the word of God, and the people of God!

As Proverbs 20:5 profoundly states, "The purpose in a man's heart is like deep water, but a man of understanding will draw it out." The Hebrew word *amoq*, translated here as "deep," literally means "exceedingly mysterious." This word aptly captures the complexity of human choices. While complexity leaves us perplexed, the proverb does not end there. Rather, the writer leads us from complexity to confidence in the second phrase of this verse. The Hebrew word *bin*, translated "understanding," literally means "discernment," "reasoning," or "skill."

During complex choices, we have the indwelling Spirit who will lead us to the word of the Lord and shape us into those who make decisions with the mind of Christ. The more we seek to align our lives with the word of God, the more we will grow in wisdom and discernment. Tools like triperspectivalism may help us toward that end, as will learning to make decisions in light of eternity.

The Timeline of Eternity

We live in a culture that assesses value and efficiency on a temporal timetable in an empirical way. When investing money, we want to know the return on the investment, the interest rate, and the amortization schedule. When choosing a school, we want to know the graduation rate and the national ranking of the potential options. When selecting a career path, we want to know the average salary, the IRA contribution rate of the company, and the insurance plan. While these are helpful and important questions to ask and answer, for the believer in Christ they are not to be the guiding factors.

As believers we know where we come from and where we are going. We know God has set eternity in the hearts of believers

(Eccles. 3:11). We know we are headed toward an eternity of worshiping and discovering God. As such, we are freed to consider the eternal, lasting outcomes of a decision rather than focus on the immediate outcomes.

Moses's life was marked by people who made decisions based on eternity. Two brave Hebrew midwives made a potentially life-threatening yet faithful decision to spare the lives of Hebrew children, despite being ordered by Pharaoh to put them to death (Ex. 1:15–20). Having little success with his first attempt to thwart the growth of God's people, Pharaoh next commanded all his people to cast every Hebrew son into the Nile River (Ex. 1:22). Yet Moses's brave and faithful mother hid him for three months before setting him in a basket on the Nile River. In confident faith, his mother sent her daughter to see how God would providentially intervene on behalf of Moses (Ex. 2:1–10). It should be no wonder to us that the man whose life had been preserved by such bold decisions would be commemorated in Hebrews 12 for his own decisions:

> By faith Moses, when he was grown up, refused to be called the son of Pharaoh's daughter, choosing rather to be mistreated with the people of God than to enjoy the fleeting pleasures of sin. He considered the reproach of Christ greater wealth than the treasures of Egypt, for he was looking to the reward. (Heb. 11:24–26)

While it is easy to read such a summary statement of a faith hero as a foregone conclusion, Moses experienced decision-making in real time, not knowing what the outcomes would be. He took an incredible risk identifying himself with his Hebrew heritage, leaving all the prestige and comforts of the Egyptian leadership into which he had been raised.

After having settled into married life at Midian as a shepherd, Moses faced another temporal decision of eternal consequence. Turning aside to investigate a strangely burning bush, Moses encountered God, who invited him into a strange new calling. Moses had to choose between the earthly comfort of the calling he had spent years perfecting and an unknown path of sure resistance and hardship. Thankfully, Moses chose the unknown way of a known God. Now every believer has him to thank for making decisions in view of eternity.

As believers who stand on the other side of the cross, we see far more clearly what Moses saw in blurry faith. Christ clearly explained to us, as to friends, the way to eternal life through him (John 14:6; 15:15). Considering this, we are invited to set all our decisions on the eternal timeline. The apostle Paul, imprisoned under the cruel Emperor Nero, awaited a sure death. Yet he wrote to Timothy, his protégé in the faith, with full confidence in the decisions he had made throughout his life. He did not experience the agony of regrets over tasks left undone or risks not taken. Rather, he said, "I have fought the good fight, I have finished the race, I have kept the faith" (2 Tim. 4:6). Having made daily decisions in light of eternity, all that was left for him was to expect the crown of righteousness to be rewarded not only to him, "but also to all who have loved his appearing" (2 Tim. 4:7–8).

The decisions made by believers living in light of eternity may perplex those whose end is this world. The cross and lives marked by the cross are "folly to those who are perishing" (1 Cor. 1:18).

However, the proverbs remind us that "the fear of the LORD is the beginning of wisdom" (Prov. 9:10).

My husband and I have dear friends who became believers in college. Both grew up near the poverty level and were determined to make a better life for themselves and their future family. In the first five years of their marriage, they allowed the job with the strongest financial security and potential to lead their choices. Then they found a church in their city. However, after a few years of gaining financially but struggling to grow spiritually, they made a bold decision. They chose to leave two lucrative positions to move to a city with a church where they knew they would be spiritually fed and challenged. After two years of an incredibly healthy church experience, they now advise younger friends to make career decisions based first on a church community. Our friends learned the hard way to place every decision on an eternal timeline. They are reaping the benefits of such an approach.

In the Sermon on the Mount, Christ taught his listeners truths that made as little earthly sense to the original audience as they do our modern ears:

Therefore, do not be anxious, saying, "What shall we eat?" or "What shall we drink?" or "What shall we wear?" For the Gentiles seek after all these things, and your heavenly Father knows that you need them all. But seek first the kingdom of God and his righteousness, and all these things will be added to you. (Matt. 6:31–33)

Jesus is not saying that food, clothing, provision, and protection do not matter. Rather, he is offering the uniquely Christian perspective of a heavenly Father whose posture is to protect and provide for his children as they trust and depend on him. We are invited to chase Christ and the eternal first rather than chase provision and protection. By setting our earthly decisions on the backdrop of eternity, we may avoid nagging regret later in life that our days and dollars were squandered rather than invested intentionally.

SWOT Analysis

A SWOT analysis is to a pros-and-cons list what a Tesla is to an electric scooter. SWOT (an acronym for *strengths, weaknesses, opportunities,* and *threats*) adds yet another nuanced tool for making decisions. As with every tool, it is only helpful when you use it. While it cannot decide for you, it can be another helpful way of slowly untying the complex knot of decisions.

Nine years ago, our family was comfortably settled in South Carolina. Extended family lived close by; we owned a home with a sprawling yard; we were members of a church we loved; we had deep relational roots. However, the Lord began to open doors for us to begin a new franchise of the college ministry we served on the West Coast. We used a SWOT analysis, among many other things, to sift through the complexities of making such a monumental move.

In the *strength* category, such a move would help reach students at San Diego State University, a campus with great needs for more Christian organizations. My husband and I both desired to live in a diverse, post-Christian city. Our children were young and about as moveable as they would ever be. A church planned to catch and house the nascent college ministry under its loving authority.

On the other hand, potential *weaknesses* abounded. The cost of living nearly tripled on the West Coast. We knew no one there. The campus was known as a "graveyard of Christian ministries." Even though San Diego was a dream location, neither of us loved the beach, nor did we care to surf.

There were ample *threats* in the form of real financial needs, family stress, and spiritual resistance. We did not need to spend too much time identifying them; they kept us up at night and on our knees wrestling in prayer. The *opportunity* list, however, grew as we grew in faith in the Lord. While our home would sizably shrink with such a move, our capacities to know and need Christ would be stretched in new and needed ways.

While the SWOT analysis did not seal our decision, the process of completing it provided a place to name and sort our jumbled thoughts and emotions. It did not solve our dilemma, but it helped steer us.

Consolation and Desolation

After having used all possible tools at our discretion and invited the input of trusted trespassers, we still may find ourselves at a difficult crossroads. We may have walked around the triangle of triperspectivalism and determined that two potential outcomes for a decision are biblical from normative perspective; feasible, helpful, and possible from a situational perspective; and desirable from an existential perspective. We may have completed a thoughtful SWOT analysis for each potential foreseeable outcome but still find ourselves stuck. What then? I wish I could say that a referee exists who might be called in to decide a close call, as happens in professional sports. But you and I both know this to be a dream.

In such situations, our desires matter. Whenever we begin to talk about feelings and desires, we land ourselves in imprecise and personal territory. It would be much easier to dismiss feelings altogether; however, God has created emotions and made us emotional creatures. We are made body, mind, and soul. As slippery as the slope may feel, our desires and emotions have a place in the decision-making process. As we discussed in chapter 4 when we explored the dashboard of decisions, desire plays a part in the decisions we make. Even though the Scriptures teach us that the heart is deceitful and not to be fully trusted (Gen. 6:5; Jer. 17:9), desire is not to be utterly discarded. Instead, in prayer and meditation, we bring our desires into the presence of God and invite his searching gaze and shaping hands (Ps. 38:9).

Rather than discard or deify our desires, we are invited to dissect them with the help of the Holy Spirit, who searches all things (1 Cor. 2:10–11). Regarding discerning the Spirit and dissecting desire, I have found the principle of consolation and desolation from Ignatius of Loyola helpful and instructive. In the spiritual exercises he wrote for the Jesuit community, Ignatius attempted to offer practices that might help practitioners experience more of God. One of the concepts he discusses is the distinction between spiritual consolation and desolation. In spiritual consolation, Ignatius refers to "every increase in hope, faith, and charity, and every interior joy which calls and attracts one toward heavenly things." Spiritual desolation, on the other hand, refers to "obtuseness of soul, turmoil within it, an impulsive motion toward low and earthy things, or disquiet from various agitations and temptations."[5] Ignatius warns that we should not make decisions when we are in a state of spiritual desolation. Any of us who have impulsively ordered something from Amazon Prime to lift our spirits can attest to his wisdom. Rather than make decisions from a desolate place, Ignatius invites the believer to wait patiently and continue to walk in the disciplines, for desolation does not last forever.

A few years ago, I found myself at a dead tie between two incredible job options. Having stayed home with my three children for over a decade, I was ready to begin a new season of employment outside the home. God opened two different potential paths before me, and it was time to decide whether I should teach at a classical Christian school or take on a role doing women's ministry at our church. We had been praying for God to make a way for my children to attend this private school, so when the principal pursued me, it seemed like a direct answer to prayer. However, the long commute and the full-time nature of the job weighed heavily on my heart. On the other hand, the part-time women's ministry role would allow my husband and me to continue to partner at a high level doing college ministry.

After weeks of praying, seeking counsel, and processing, I felt like we had made no ground. Every few hours, my heart would flip back and forth, leaving me dizzy and confused. Finally, a friend reminded me of consolation and desolation. She asked, "When you think about teaching at the school, how do you feel?"

After peeling back a few layers of what felt like the right thing to say, I began to be gut-level honest with both myself and my friend. The thought of waking up so early to fight traffic and teach other people's children made me feel tired and anxious. Imagining myself in that teaching role, my heart felt bifurcated and pulled in two directions. Yet when asked the same question about the women's ministry role, my heart felt relieved and even excited. The thought of writing curriculum and teaching God's word to women made my heart soar, while the thought of teaching at the school made my heart sink. Both would have honored God. Both were feasible and helpful to my family in diverse ways. Both included cost and risk. But only one of them left my soul consoled.

Feelings are not ultimate in the decision-making process, but they do have a role to play, especially after decisions have been bathed in prayer and pressed through the sieve of Scripture. However, Ignatius's principle of consolation and desolation is a tool, not biblical truth. Like any tool, it is best used in the proper context for the proper purpose. I offer this tool with caution and careful instruction because there will be plenty of times when God calls us to do things that don't feel comfortable or easy.

The Garden of Gethsemane

God often calls us to do hard things. After all, we follow Christ, who told his disciples, "Whoever does not take his cross and follow me is not worthy of me" (Matt. 10:38). If we only and always choose the familiar and the comfortable, we will miss out on the rewards of the gospel. If we are truly seeking to obey God's will, we will learn to hold our own wills loosely and with open hands. In the words of Elisabeth Elliot, "If our hands are full of our own plans, there isn't room to receive His."[6]

However, believers are not called to seek hardship for the sake of hardship. Sometimes in making decisions, we can get the wrong idea that to be a follower of Christ means we must always choose the hardest, most unappealing way. The God who created us with unique preferences, passions, and gifts is not a hard master, though his way is often hard. He uses hard seasons and experiences to shape and prune us into his likeness. Those who have experienced extreme hardships often say that they wouldn't trade that for anything. They say this, not because they are gluttons for punishment, but because they have experienced more of Jesus through these hardships. The hard way became to them a hallowed way because of the nearness and presence of Jesus.

In the quiet garden on the night before his excruciating death, Christ wrestled in prayer and pain to the point of bursting blood vessels in his face, which caused him to sweat blood. In these moments, he was honest with his father about his preferences and desires. He begged, "My Father, it if be possible, let this cup pass from me; nevertheless, not as I will, but as you will" (Matt. 26:39). He did not gleefully, glibly choose the way of the cross; however, after earnestly expressing his desire that there be an easier way, Christ submitted to the Father's will in adoring acquiescence.

In fact, the writer of Hebrews clearly tells us that Christ endured the cross and its unthinkable pain and shame "for the joy that was set before him" (Heb. 12:2). If God calls us to do hard things or directs us to choose an uncomfortable way, he does so in order to give us greater reward. While that reward might not be felt instantaneously, his precious and very great promises assure us that light and momentary afflictions are producing for us an eternal weight of glory (2 Cor. 4:16–18). As an aging Peter tenderly told his suffering flock of believers, we can rejoice even when "grieved by various trials" because "the tested genuineness" of our faith "may be found to result in praise and glory and honor at the revelation of Jesus Christ" (1 Pet. 1:6–7).

7

You've Decided, So Now What?

RELIEF AND CONFIDENCE OFTEN immediately follow when we have finally made a tough decision. After spending days, weeks, or maybe even months gathering information, listening to counsel, and processing with the Lord in prayer, we've finally come to the decision. We have signed the job contract, placed the down-payment on the home, or gone through the church membership class.

While I wish I could say those moments of relief on the other side of decision-making steadily remain, they are often followed by a triad of enemies: doubt, fear, and regret. "What if" questions pop into our minds at the most inopportune times. *What if I chose to become a member at the wrong church? What if I joined the wrong sorority? What if I chose the wrong major? What if I bought a home in the wrong neighborhood? What if I was missing a very important piece of information when I made my decision? What if I thought I was listening to the Lord's guidance, but I was really chasing the approval of my trusted advisors?*

In addition to our natural propensity to doubt decisions previously made in faith, our culture adds another element: fear of missing out. *What if there is an option with better pay, better friends, better outcomes, or more enjoyment that I am missing?* Rather than enabling us to walk with our gazes fixed on Jesus, the founder and perfecter of our faith, we end up looking around frantically and fearfully (see Heb. 12:1–3).

Fearful Frames and a Firm God

Fear steals focus from God's ability and wisdom, wrongfully placing a myopic focus on self. Through fear, self looms so large that we begin to believe that one decision can throw off God's plan. Fear shrinks our infinite God and enlarges self in a way that robs God of glory and ourselves of peace. Fear forgets that the same God who spoke galaxies into existence holds our lives together. Fear forgets that "he is before all things, and in him all things hold together" (Col. 1:17).

Thankfully, God knows the frames of his fragile and fear-filled people. We are not alone in our battles against fear, doubt, and regret. Throughout the Scriptures, God continually reminds his forgetful people to fear not. When Abram was crippled with doubt about the decision to refuse an earthly reward, the Lord came to him in a vision, saying "Fear not, Abram, I am your shield; your reward shall be very great" (Gen. 15:1).

Later when Moses's fear threatens to keep him from walking in obedience to confront Pharaoh, God takes the time to reason with him, reminding him of his intention to provide for and go ahead of his chosen servant (Ex. 4:11, 14). When an aged Moses finally passed the leadership baton on to Joshua, the new leader was understandably terrified, having big sandals to fill. Joshua was likely questioning Moses's choice of him, wondering if there might be someone more qualified. God, intimately aware of the fears plaguing the future leader, coaxed Joshua toward courage, saying, "Have I not commanded you? Be strong and courageous. Do not be frightened, and do not be dismayed, for the LORD your God is with you wherever you go" (Josh. 1:9).

As such, we should not be surprised that the incarnate Christ often sang the same tune to his similarly fearful and doubting disciples. When Christ formally called Simon Peter to discipleship, Peter initially responded in great fear and trepidation. Christ responded, "Do not be afraid; from now on you will be catching men" (Luke 5:10). Timothy, the apostle Paul's spiritual son and mentee, was prone to fearfulness and timidity. Like Joshua who had succeeded Moses, Timothy felt the weight of the mantle being placed on his shoulders. However, Paul reminded him that God had not given him a spirit of fear but "of power and love and self-control" (2 Tim.1:7).

Corrie ten Boom knew a thing or two about fear and worry as one who lived through the Nazi occupation of Holland and made hard decisions to hide Jewish families in her home. She had ample reason to worry but learned, experience by experience, that worrying about the future did not change it. Rather, she learned from her faithful father Casper ten Boom that God will give us just what we need just when we need it. In a moment of worry, he told her, "Our wise Father in heaven knows when we are going to need things, too. Don't run ahead of Him, Corrie."[1] We, like Corrie, need to be gently reminded not to run ahead of our faithful Father.

Taking Thoughts Captive

Paul wisely recognized the inverse correlation between fear and self-control. When we allow fears to run amuck in our hearts, minds, and lives, they rob us of the peace Christ purchased for us. Paul urged the believers at Colossae, "Let the peace of Christ rule in your hearts" (Col. 3:15). The Greek word *brabeuō*, translated "rule," literally means to act as an umpire or an arbiter. Paul borrowed this word from the Greek games with which his readers would have been familiar. The image invoked is that of a referee stepping into a human heart where fears and truth are wrestling for ascendency to create order.

When doubts, fears, and regrets crowd in upon the spaces of our souls, the word of God and the character of God are meant to act as referees, throwing fears back to the sidelines and preserving the peace that we have in Christ. When speaking to the Corinthian church, Paul uses another powerful image regarding unwanted thoughts and fears and mindsets. Paul writes, "We destroy arguments and every lofty opinion raised against the knowledge of God, and take every thought captive to obey Christ" (2 Cor. 10:5). Taking errant thoughts captive sounds simple, but wrangling wayward fears and niggling doubts requires hard work. Oftentimes it is far easier to let the fears and doubts control us than it is to control and subdue them under the dominion of Christ. However, fears will rob us of strength and joy as they steal our attention from the purposes God has intended for the present day.

When we begin to doubt the goodness of God or his ability to providentially steer our lives, it is helpful to consider the very nature of our God. As Paul so powerfully reasoned with the Romans, "If God is for us, who can be against us?" (Rom. 8:31). Having provided his Son for our greatest need, will we choose to doubt his ability to provide for us in the smaller things (Rom. 8:32)? If God can work beauty out of the cross through resurrection, can we not trust him to work good through our past decisions?

Fear of Missing Out

Comparison and covetousness are not new to humanity. They have reared their ugly heads since the fall of mankind into sin. From the very first pair of siblings, Cain and Abel, comparison and competition have pulled our gaze from the Lord to those around us in envy (Gen. 4:1–7). When God established the principles of life for his people Israel, he made a commandment against covetousness (Gen. 20:17). He knows how quickly our eyes and our hearts look around rather than up for contentment and security.

Sometimes after making a decision that has left us feeling confident and called, we begin to look around in doubt, fear, and insecurity. Like Peter after he had listened to the Lord's clear call to step out of the boat and onto the water, we are doing well until we lose our focal point (Matt. 14:28–33). Looking around at our circumstances or surveying the circumstances of others, we may begin to drown in doubt or freeze in fear that we are missing out on something better. If this happened when people's lives were limited to small, local settings, how much more does the flattening of the globe through the Internet invite such temptation?

The enemy of our souls would love to steal the freedom, peace, and confidence that Christ has purchased for his people (John 10:10). Our flesh loves to give lingering, covetous looks at the lives of others. After being graciously reinstated by the resurrected Jesus, Peter likely felt relieved and joyful. Directly after Christ had hinted at the way Peter's life would end and bidding him yet again, "Follow me," Peter immediately diverted his gaze and attention to his friend John, asking, "Lord, what about this man?" (John 21:18–23). This encounter always makes me smile because it so closely resembles my own experiences. Once we have finally decided and settled into the circumstances that God has ordained for us, no sooner do we begin to look around in comparison and competition. We wonder if someone else made a better choice or received a better set of consequences or rewards.

Jesus's response to Peter still speaks to us today, "If it is my will that he remain until I come, what is that to you? You follow me!" (John 21:22). Likewise Psalms 16; 37; and 73 offer helpful soul instruction to those who struggle with fear of missing out. The moments and even months after we have made a decision provide many opportunities to continually lift our eyes to our Maker in faith and expectant trust.

Poor Decisions

My nine-year-old son stood with his bicycle at the top of the steep hill in front of our house. His gaggle of neighborhood friends stood at the base of the hill where my husband and I were doing some gardening. Suddenly my son cried out from the top of the hill, "Hey guys, watch this!"

My husband and I immediately looked up in alarm, as those are dangerous words coming from a young boy. Much to our surprise, our son's next move was not to ride down the hill on the bike but to send the bike down the hill without a rider. Our eyes moved back and forth between the bike, which was picking up speed, and the new-to-us car toward which it was headed. Sure enough, the bike slammed into the side of the car as we watched in shock and horror. My son, recognizing what he had done and not even understanding himself why he had done it, began running down the hill. I fully expected him to run to his room in embarrassment, but he did something we did not expect. He ran directly into my husband's arms, paying my husband one of the greatest compliments of his life. In a moment when fear of shame and consequences might have made him run *from* his father, he chose to run *to* his arms. He knew his father well enough to know that there would surely be consequences, but he also knew that his father loved him far more than he was disappointed with him.

Life is a long, complex series of decisions. Even those who have the indwelling Holy Spirit and the word of God to direct them will make wrong or unwise decisions. Our maturity as a believer is not measured by how often we make wrong decisions but how we respond when we do. Both Judas and Peter made terrible mistakes in the last days of Jesus's life on earth. Both followed Jesus closely as disciples and friends. Both sat under the same teaching. Both made poor decisions in those critical days before the cross. Both betrayed Jesus. Only one repented and was restored to Christ. Our responses to wrong choices, be they tremendous or tiny, decide the trajectory of our lives.

The Generous Father

No matter how many wrong decisions we have made, we are always only one decision away from our heavenly Father's arms.

A pastor in my formative spiritual years once mentioned that every step east of Eden makes the next eastward step a little easier. Here, movement east of Eden represents volitional choices that move us further and further away from God's design for his people and his world. While it is true that certain wrong choices aid and abet other subsequent wrong choices, it is significant for God's people to remember they are always one step from nearness to their perfect Father.

In seeking to explain the heavenly Father's disposition toward his children, Jesus employed the use of a powerful story, the parable of the prodigal son. This label, "prodigal son," is a misnomer, because it is more truly the story of the generous father and his relationship to his two sons. Both of his children made choices to separate themselves from their father. While the elder brother made moral choices to be the good, hardworking son, his self-righteousness kept him from experiencing deeper intimacy with his dad. Though he was close physically, his proximity did not equate to intimacy. The younger son, meanwhile, had chosen the path of outright, obvious rebellion. He asked for his part of the inheritance while the father was still alive, essentially wishing him dead. Then, taking his inheritance, he chose to walk away and live as if his father were dead to him.

The younger son made a series of increasingly poor decisions that eventually landed him as a hired hand. He was so hungry he longed to join the pigs at the trough for dinner. He had taken many steps east of Eden without even realizing how far from his true home he had wandered physically, emotionally, and relationally. In that critical low moment, he took a step that brought him back toward his father, saying, "How many of my father's hired servants have more than enough bread, but I perish here with hunger! I will arise and go to my father" (Luke 15:17–18).

Just as each step toward sin strengthens the next step in that direction, each step toward repentance and restoration strengthens the trip westward back toward Eden. The repentant son did not have only a fleeting moment of remorse and sadness. He put the remorse and sadness into clear and brave action when he started walking home. I am certain that along the long way, he had plenty of time to wrestle with the weight of his decisions and to wonder how his father would respond. All those imagined outcomes were erased when he saw his father running to him from a long way off. The father was eagerly awaiting his son's return. We do not know how many days or years passed between the son's rude departure and repentant return. We simply know that, while the son was still a tiny ant in the distance, the father recognized him and ran to meet him. Rather than chide his son, he caressed him. Rather than point his finger at him, he put a ring on his son's finger as a token of love.

While this story paints the picture of an extravagant earthly father, the reality of our heavenly Father is even more extravagant. There was one Son, the perfect Son of God, who always perfectly obeyed the heavenly Father, living in intimate, obedient dependence upon him. He always made choices considering his Father's will and ways. He lived under the gaze of his good Father. In his obedience, he did not separate himself from his Father in pride. That Son was not rescued. His robes were ripped from him as people mocked him. His feet were nailed to a tree. He was the lamb that was slaughtered so that we could be met with love by our heavenly Father.

Keep Looking at Aslan

My youngest son is finally at the age where we can read the Chronicles of Narnia together, which is a verifiable rite of passage in our home. Even though I have read *The Lion, the Witch, and the Wardrobe* more times than I can count, something new never fails to grab my heart every time I read it.

During a recent reading, I was struck by Aslan's quiet, calm reinstatement of the treacherous Edmund. The gracious reception of Edmund by Peter, Susan, and Lucy after he had so clearly put them and all Narnia at risk also grabbed my attention. Edmund might easily have been tempted to self-flagellate after he had snuck away to sell out his brother and sisters to the deceptive White Witch, lured by false promises of Turkish delight and power. However, Aslan's interaction with Edmund after his rescue from the clutches of the witch had none of the scent of shame or punishment that he expected:

> As soon as they [Peter, Susan, and Lucy] had breakfasted they all went out, and there they saw Aslan and Edmund walking together in the dewy grass, apart from the rest of the court. There is no need to tell you (and no one ever heard) what Aslan was saying, but it was a conversation which Edmund never forgot. As the others drew nearer Aslan turned to meet them, bringing Edmund with him.
>
> "Here is your brother," he said, "and—there is no need to talk to him about what is past."[2]

Later, the White Witch attempts to harm the reinstated Edmund by reminding him of his poor decisions. However, Edmund refuses to let her injure him with her reminders:

> Edmund had got past thinking about himself after all he'd been through and after the talk he'd had that morning. He just went on looking at Aslan. It didn't seem to matter what the witch said.[3]

When we realize that we have made a poor choice, no matter how large or small the stakes may seem, we can learn from the returning son to run to the Father, and from Edmund to keep our eyes on Aslan.

Everyone loves a few evenings to relax and unwind. However, if the Spirit convicts us that we have been wasting too many free evenings binge-watching a favorite show, the best response is to admit our poor decision and take it to the forgiving Father, asking for better discernment for the following free evening.

On a larger scale, if we have made a poor decision to purchase a car when the old car, while dented, still operates flawlessly, we can follow the same path of action. While the consequences for that decision may be greater, the character of the Father remains the same.

If we have chosen a church or job based more on comfort and crowd-think than on the basis of God's word, we are invited to admit our misuse of secondary gauges and reevaluate, considering more lasting priorities. We are also invited to learn from our mistakes so that in the future we will rely more on God's direction than upon fleeting impressions.

Because of the gospel, our identity is not the sum of our decisions but the sum of Christ's perfect decisions. This incredibly freeing reality, rather than pressing us toward carelessness in our decisions, is intended to compel us toward greater faithfulness as image bearers of God.

Wise Decisions

Thankfully, by God's great grace, we can make wise decisions. Just as our responses to poor decisions reveal our maturity in Christ, our responses to wise decisions are also windows into our hearts.

While the world's response to wise decision-making tends to be marked by pride in self, the believer is invited to boast in the goodness of the Lord. Rather than viewing wise decisions as trophies or monuments to our own awesomeness, we are invited to string such decisions together as a record of God's faithfulness and a reminder of his character. Such records of God's faithfulness can be used to help us fight fear and unbelief in future decision-making scenarios.

To his disciples who were in danger of becoming puffed up and proud of their discipleship and costly obedience to him, Christ said, "When you have done all that you were commanded, say, 'We are unworthy servants; we have only done what was our duty'" (Luke 17:10).

While these words may sound harsh to us, they are Christ's gracious way of protecting his disciples from pride and its perverse effects. Christ knows the propensity of human hearts toward self-reliance and self-congratulation. He also knows the propensity toward self-hatred and self-deprecation after a poor decision has been made. He offered them and still offers us an alternative route that leads to deeper reliance upon and worship of the Father.

Similarly, when the apostle Paul looked back on his life of intense faithfulness and costly obedience to the Lord, he chose to press ahead toward greater faithfulness rather than look back upon his spiritual resume in pride and satisfaction. He told his friends at Philippi, "Not that I have already obtained this or am already perfect, but I press on to make it my own, because Christ Jesus has made me his own" (Phil. 3:12). Rather than proudly gazing upon his wise decisions postconversion, Paul set his mind on more of Christ. He resolved to "press on toward the goal for the prize of the upward call of God in Christ Jesus" (Phil. 3:14).

Later in life, a friend of Corrie ten Boom recounted something she had told him that forever changed his approach to compliments and moments of obedience and victory in the Christian life:

> When people come up and give me a compliment—"Corrie, that was a good talk," or "Corrie, you were so brave," I take each remark as if it were a flower. At the end of each day, I lift up the bouquet of flowers I have gathered throughout the day and say, "Here you are, Lord, it is all yours."[4]

Following Corrie's example, when we have made a wise decision or a series of wise decisions, let us offer those gifts back to the Father, who enabled them.

The Psalms as Patterns of Praise

Since they were written and gathered, the psalms have provided God's people with a pattern of prayer and worship for various seasons and situations of life. The more we read and meditate upon them, the more these Spirit-inspired songs and prayers will shape our own hearts.

While there are countless examples of prayers of thanksgiving toward God, Psalm 34 exemplifies a God-honoring boasting. While the author of the psalm, David, had great reason to boast as one who had slain Goliath and been anointed as the future king of Israel, he knew from whom his strength came. Rather than use his escape from Abimelech (which was the occasion for this psalm) to boast in himself, David used the occasion to invite others into the goodness of the God who takes care of those who trust in him.

In addition to the more well-known psalms of thanksgiving (Pss. 45; 117; 118; and 138), other beautiful songs of remembrance and thanks are scattered throughout the Scriptures. These songs serve the twofold purpose of remembering God's past faithfulness and passing those stories along to the coming generations who need to be reminded of the nature of their God. The Song of Moses in Exodus 15, Hannah's prayer in 1 Samuel 2, and Mary's prayer known as the Magnificat in Luke 1 provide both devotional fodder and instructional examples of giving praise back to the one to whom it is due. On the heels of God-enabled obedience through faith, Moses, Hannah, and Mary show us how to point ourselves back to the nature of God.

Remembering and Rehearsing

God, being very God, knows the nature of his often-forgetful people. He knows how easily fear can grip us and how quickly we forget his past faithfulness when looking into an unknown future. As such, God threaded the idea of remembrance into the very life of his people. At Mount Sinai, God commanded his people to observe weekly Sabbaths and yearly feasts such as the Passover. In practicing the Passover every year, God's people were forced to remember the miraculous and marvelous ways he had heard their cries and rescued them from slavery in Egypt. In the smells and tastes of the Seder meal, they rehearsed and remembered their bondage and inability to free themselves. They saw a lamb bone that reminded them of the blood of the spotless lamb slain that death might pass over them.

If God's people were to take such intricate and intentional care to remember his faithfulness in rescuing them from physical slavery, how much more are the children of God called to remember his ultimate rescue of us from our slavery to sin through the spotless Lamb to which all the former Passover lambs had pointed?

The fourth commandment is known as the "blessed commandment." Only a good God would command his people to observe a day of rest. The Sabbath forced God's people to remember that he, not they, were the center. In the Sabbath, work and activity ceased to a near halt to remind God's people that, while they were finite, dependent, and limited, he was infinite, independent, and unlimited. The forced rest gave God's people time to remember and rejoice over his salvation, provision, and protection of them. Looking back on the past week, they were to give God praise; looking ahead to the next week, they were to look to him to give strength, wisdom, and perspective.

The Sabbath practice looks different for believers. Christ himself told his disciples who were being ridiculed for not practicing the Jewish Sabbath traditions, "The Son of Man is lord of the Sabbath" (Matt. 12:8). However, Sabbath rhythms still provide much-needed spaces and placeholders to remember and rehearse God's faithfulness to us. Without these regular rhythms of resting to remember, our hearts get misaligned. We forget that even our obedience is a good gift given and enabled by the Father of lights in whom there is no shadow or variation due to change (James 1:17). Regular rhythms of remembering and rehearsing God's faithfulness in the past enable us to better trust him with present and future decisions.

On the other side of decisions stands God, who is the same yesterday and today and forever (Heb. 13:8). When doubts, fears, or regrets threaten to steal our joy, we look to his word. When we have made a poor decision, we repent and return to his arms. When we have made a decision that honors him, we give him the praise, remembering his past faithfulness for future hope.

The Next Right Thing

The relief that comes from making one decision, while real, is ephemeral. Soon after making one decision, we are likely to face our next. If our peace comes only when we have finally decided, it will be sporadic at best. God offers us peace throughout the entire series of big and small decisions that compound to make a life. The present moment invites us to present faithfulness.[5] When we become overwhelmed day to day, we are reminded to faithfully do the next thing God sets in front of us. A faithful minute becomes a faithful day, which becomes a faithful week, which becomes a faithful year. In the words of Thomas Carlyle, "Do thy first duty. The second will become clear."[6]

Conclusion

The Destination of Decisions

WE BEGAN OUR JOURNEY together in the thick fog of decision-making. Dizzied by the ubiquitous choices around us and confused by conflicting voices informing our decisions, we lifted our eyes to one who designed us as decision makers in his image.

In the first half of the book, we did the hard and often underappreciated work of laying a theological foundation for decision-making. Resisting the urge to jump directly to practice, we wrestled with the perceived tension between God's sovereignty and our responsibility in making decisions. We explored the biblical range of meaning for the will of God (his decrees, his preferences, his providences, and his specific will in certain situations). We learned that God's will for us is that we become like him (1 Thess. 4:3). God has given us incredible freedom in making decisions, so long as we keep within the bounds of the moral law he has given us. While we would rather have a map, God has given us a guide in the person of the Holy Spirit, who illuminates the revealed word of God to us and leads us toward applied wisdom.

In the second half of the book, we approached decisions prag-
matically. After familiarizing ourselves with the dashboards by
which we make decisions, we set the stage with practical preparation for decision-making. Using the analogy of gathering puzzle
pieces, we learned pivotal pieces for making decisions (passions,
priorities, and providential circumstances). Most importantly, we
underscored the primary roles prayer and fasting play in preparation for making decisions, be they tiny or tremendous. John
Frame's triperspectivalism taught us a three-pronged approach to
evaluating our choices (normative, situational, and existential).
The Ignatian concept of consolation and desolation gave us a lens
for processing emotions in difficult decisions. While feelings have
a role to play, we learned obedience from Jesus in the garden of
Gethsemane.

We rounded out our journey by addressing the fear, regret,
and doubt that sometimes crop up on the other side of major
decisions. We explored scriptures inviting us to take our thoughts
captive to the obedience of Christ (2 Cor. 10:5; Col. 3:15) and
learned how to process both wise and unwise decisions. Finally,
we remembered that God's faithfulness in past decisions propels
us toward present faithfulness and future hope.

The Destination

It is natural to get lost in an episodic adventure saga, whether an
ancient classic like Homer's *Odyssey* or a more modern classic like
Twain's *Huckleberry Finn*. We get so engaged in one leg of the long
journey that we nearly forget the overarching tale and the ultimate
destination. We are so anxious to see Odysseus survive the Sirens,
the monsters, and the whirlpool that we abruptly find ourselves

back home with him. We so enjoy the shenanigans on the raft with Huck and Jim that we find ourselves surprised when they arrive home different people. It tends to be the same with decisions. We get so easily lost in the individual chapters of our decision-making stories that we forget to fix our eyes on the destination. Ample drama and tension at each curve keep our attention on the path rather than the destination. However, our decisions are moving us toward a destination just as surely as Homer and Twain are steering their protagonists toward their own.

Ivan Ilyich focused on each decision as it approached him. He married into the right class, bought the right house, and pursued the right career. However, he never stopped to consider the destination toward which these decisions were leading him. When he finally considered his destination, he was already on his deathbed. It was too late. His decisions were made, his destination decided.

Two Accolades

The Scriptures invite us to keep the destination in mind as we make daily decisions. Just as surely as we shape our decisions, our decisions shape us. As believers, imagining the day when we will hear God say to us, "Well done, good and faithful servant," ought to shape the way we make decisions today. Living for the day when we will hear, "Enter into the joy of your master," ought to inform the decisions of today (Matt. 25:21–23).

C. S. Lewis defines *glory* as the pure "satisfaction of having pleased those whom I rightly loved and rightly feared."[1] Defined as such, the ultimate destination of our decisions as believers is to please the Father. When we receive the divine accolade, we will be like humble children pleased to know the Father is pleased with us. In that moment, all the hours spent waiting, wrestling, and wading through decisions will be forgotten. The anguish and anxiety of decisions will be swallowed in adoration of our Savior and delight in his presence. Keeping one eye on the ultimate destination of our decisions and one eye on the immediate decisions set before us, we walk faithfully toward the full presence of the Father.

While I look forward to hearing the divine accolade, I equally look forward to another phrase being spoken over my life. Two days before Jesus's death, when he was resting at his friends' home in Bethany, "a woman came with an alabaster flask of ointment of pure nard, very costly, and she broke the flask and poured it over his head" (Mark 14:3). Some of his closest friends who were present, indignant at her action and thinking it an extravagant waste, scolded her (Mark 14:4). However, Christ came powerfully and tenderly to her defense, saying, "Leave her alone. Why do you trouble her? She has done a beautiful thing. . . . She has done what she could" (Mark 14:6–8).

The world and even the disciples looked upon her choice as a waste. Yet Christ saw something different. With gentle words Christ spoke over this woman whose gratitude came from her deep sense of need. It is far easier for me to identify myself with this sinful yet loved woman than the two servants who made wise decisions to invest their talents. I know my frailty. I know the decisions I have made in the past. I know the power of my flesh and the weakness of my spirit (Matt. 26:41). I know the depths to which fear of man and desire for human approval have shaped and still shape my decisions. It feels like a stretch to see myself as a good, faithful servant, but I can see myself in the sinful woman.

We cannot make perfect decisions, but we can fall at the feet of our Master when in need. We will not always act in wisdom, but we can worship the one who did. While we may not be able to pour out our alabaster jars in one intense moment of appreciation and anointing, we can worship Jesus through our daily decisions. Drip by drip, day by day, our decisions can lead us to the day when we hear, "Well done," and, "She has done what she could!"

I still wish we could sit down for that cup of coffee to process the decision(s) that brought you to this book. While that remains impossible, I eagerly expect and hope you will sit down with a trusted trespasser to discuss and digest these pages. Even more significantly, I pray that the decision-making process draws you closer to the one who designed you to make decisions. May he lead you and conform you more into his image and likeness until the day when decisions culminate in the delight of his presence.

Acknowledgments

GLORY TO GOD! He has dealt graciously with me. As early as I can remember, I have dreamed of writing a book. In my imaginings, such a process was quiet and solitary and happened in seclusion in the woods, as with Thoreau; however, writing a book has been far more humbling and communal than I envisioned. It seems God wanted to teach me yet again the principle that he enjoys the process of molding and shaping us as much as the product itself. If it were not for the incredible community God has provided, this book would not exist.

For my husband and best friend, G'Joe: so much of this book's contents came from your wisdom and discipleship. You champion me in ways that I do not deserve. You carve out time for me to write and think. Most importantly, you point me to Jesus. Next to responding to Jesus's initiation toward me, marrying you remains the most significant decision I have ever made.

For my children, Tyus, Eli, and Phin: you have allowed me to take over our kitchen table with books and to sneak away for a few hours every week to write. You have encouraged me when I was overwhelmed, folded laundry for me, and prayed for me. I am so thankful that God entrusted you to us. Being your mother is one of the greatest callings of my life.

For Dave DeWit, Megan Hill, Melissa Kruger, Lydia Brownback, and the teams at Crossway and TGC: you patiently coached and gently guided me through the writing process. Your wisdom and grace have made this opportunity one I will never forget. May your investments be multiplied for the glory of God!

For Linda Kim, Wendy Willard, Tyler Velin, Steven Cooper, and my other dear friends who prayed for this entire process: your prayers, your eyes, and your edits helped shape this manuscript. Your wit and wisdom have made rough drafts far less rough.

For my family and the long list of friends and mentors who have walked with me through all of life's decisions from the earliest years to the present: your lives, influences, and decisions have providentially shaped me. Thank you!

Study Questions

Introduction

1. Consider what led you to read this book. What decisions are you facing? What are you hoping to learn?

2. Describe a major decision you have made in the past. What informed your decision? What emotions did you experience throughout the process? What were some of the consequences of that decision?

3. Describe a time when you experienced anxiety as the dizziness of freedom.

4. When you think about the most significant decisions, what decisions come immediately to heart and mind?

5. In your opinion, what role do daily habits play in shaping our lives? Name five habits that deeply shape your life.

Chapter 1: The Drama of Decisions

1. Think about your favorite book, movie, or program. Around what central decisions does the action revolve?

2. Consider the context in which you live. Which of the three modern approaches to decision-making (New Age divination, reason alone, follow your heart) most describe the way you and those around you approach decision-making? What are the dangers of this approach?

3. In her book *Walking on Water*, Madeleine L'Engle wrote, "It is the ability to choose which makes us human."[1] Explain why you agree or disagree with her statement.

4. Decisions necessarily involve the mystery of God's sovereignty and man's responsibility. Describe a time when you relied too heavily on one or the other in the process of making a major decision.

5. Read 2 Corinthians 5:17 and Romans 8:1–4. "In Christ, we are no longer judged on the sum of our disobedient decisions but on the sum of his obedient decisions" (p. 30). What past decisions haunt you, causing condemnation? How does the gospel change the way you see these decisions?

6. Read 2 Chronicles 20:12 and Psalm 62:8. What do these passages teach us about the dilemmas in our lives? What decisions in your life (or the lives of those you love) are causing drama in your heart currently? Spend time praying through these decisions with a trusted friend.

Further Study

Choose one of the following biblical figures: Noah (Gen. 6:9–22; 7:1–5), Abraham (Gen. 12:1–9; 22:1–8), or Hannah (1 Samuel 1). Reread the suggested Scriptures pertaining to their lives through the lens of decisions. What decisions did they face? Where can you trace both God's sovereignty and man's responsibility in their lives?

Chapter 2: The Design of Decisions

1. We live in an Amazon Prime culture. As such, we have grown to expect rapid processes. Describe a time when you experienced a lengthy process that was worth the wait. What made the process challenging? What made the process enjoyable?

2. The chapter mentions Mary and Jehoshaphat as those who grew in intimacy with the Lord through the process of making decisions. What other biblical figures experienced intimacy with the Lord through the process of making significant decisions? What can we learn from them?

3. Read Galatians 6:7–8. What can we learn about the law of reaping and sowing (choice and consequence) from this passage? How does grace fit into the reality of choice and consequence? Where in the Scriptures have you seen consequences meted out with grace? Where have you experienced this in your own life?

4. As you look back over past decisions, what have you learned from their respective consequences? How have those past decisions shaped the way you approach decisions in the present?

5. Are there small habits that have led to massive mistakes in your past? Where have you seen the mercy of God even amid real consequences?

6. Read Job 38 and Job 42:1–6. How do the rhetorical questions posed by God create a healthy, right fear of God? What is Job's response to God in Job 42? When you think of the fear of God, what comes to heart and mind? What is the difference between filial fear and servile fear? How does filial fear shape the decisions we face?

Further Study

Read the short book of Ruth in the Old Testament. First, imagine the decisions that Ruth and Naomi faced from their perspectives. Next, trace God's providential dealings with Naomi and Ruth. How does this book lead you to worship God? How does it change the way you see the circumstances and decisions you are presently facing?

Chapter 3: Theological Foundations for Decisions

1. Consider a time when you were seeking to discern God's will for a particular choice. How did you go about seeking God's will? What tools or principles guided your seeking?

2. When you think about God's will, what comes to mind (hidden or revealed will)? Why do you think we spend so much time wanting to know his hidden will when we know so much of his revealed will?

3. Read Romans 8:28–30, which describes God's providential guidance of his people. Describe a time when you were able to see God work all things together for good in a difficult decision.

4. As much as we want a formula or an effortless way to divine God's will, God has better plans for believers on the other side of the life, death, and resurrection of Christ. Sometimes making decisions by walking the way of biblical wisdom feels like a problem rather than a privilege. Why does this mode of making decisions frustrate us? How does it elevate us and sanctify us?

5. Read Deuteronomy 29:29. What secret things do you wish you knew right now? Where is God calling you to obey revealed things currently?

6. How does an understanding of the three types of law (ceremonial, civil, and moral) guide us in making decisions?

Further Study

Read 1 Thessalonians 4:1–8. What do we learn about God's will from this passage? How does this description of God's will inform or change the way you think about the decisions you make daily?

Chapter 4: The Dashboard of Decisions

1. Which of the three cultures (shame-honor, guilt-innocence, or fear-power) have primarily and secondarily shaped you? How has your primary cultural experience shaped your past decisions?

2. Read Jonah 2:8 and 1 John 5:21. Why do you think both Jonah and John warned people about idolatry? Our hearts are idol-making factories. Which idols most inform your decisions? Describe a time when an idol had an oversized voice in a decision you made. What was the outcome of that decision?

3. When have you experienced the "tyranny of the urgent" in the past few weeks? What practically helps you live more in quadrant 2 (the important, but not urgent)?

4. Read Psalm 139:23–24 and Jeremiah 17:9. Why do we need to invite the Lord to search our hearts and test our desires? Consider a decision you are currently facing. What desires are underneath this decision? How are these desires right and good? Where are these desires deceitful and misleading?

5. What other gauges are missing from the dashboard of decisions?

6. The gospel changes everything. For those who are in Christ, the gospel gauge informs and right-sizes all other gauges. Compare and contrast a major life decision before your gospel gauge was intact with one made afterward.

Further Study

Read Isaiah 44. Compare and contrast the idols God's people worshiped and the one true God. What words describe idols and idolatry? What words describe God? Consider what idols you may be looking to and spend time confessing them to the Lord. Next, read Psalm 104. Make a list of the things the psalmist attributes to God and spend time praising God for his character.

Chapter 5: Practical Preparation for Decisions

1. Which of the three proper expectations for making decisions (clarity, complexity, Christ, the pioneer) is most helpful to you? Why?

2. Frederick Buechner wrote, "The place where God calls you to is the place where your deep gladness and the world's deep hunger meet."[2] What are some of the deep passions and places of deep gladness God has placed inside your heart? If you don't know, ask some trusted trespassers what they see in you.

3. Consider your present season of life. What are your top priorities in this season? How do these priorities inform the decisions you are making currently? How have these priorities changed from a previous season of your life?

4. Read Psalm 16. Describe the providential circumstances of your present lot.

5. Read Proverbs 11:14; 12:15; and 19:20–21. What do these proverbs teach us about our need for trusted counselors? Who are your trusted trespassers? Describe a time when a friend challenged you or spoke with grace and truth into your life. Describe a time when a friend helped you to see your blind spots.

6. Honestly describe your daily and weekly intake of God's word. What habits in your life are training you to listen to the Lord?

How often you are talking about the decisions you are facing as compared to how often you are praying over them?

Further Study

Plan an appropriate fast (e.g., food, social media, coffee) and ask a friend to hold you accountable to this plan. As you fast, spend time praying through and meditating upon Psalm 42 and/or Psalm 84.

Chapter 6: Practical Paradigms for Decisions

1. Read Isaiah 40:21–26. What can we learn about God from this passage? We are limited in our perspective and wisdom, but thankfully our God is both unlimited and omniperspectival. How does this reality change the way you approach decisions?

2. Practice pressing a situation or decision through the triperspectival framework (normative, situational, existential).

3. In the moment, it is easy to become myopic about decisions or dilemmas we are facing. What helps you place decisions and current circumstances on the timeline of eternity? What happens when you do not?

4. Think about a decision you are deliberating (or anticipate you may have to decide in the future). Take a few moments to evaluate the various options using the SWOT tool (strengths, weaknesses, opportunities, threats). What insights do you glean?

5. Consider a decision you are facing in the present. How are you holding your own plans regarding that decision (fist closed,

holding tightly, holding loosely, etc.)? Why do you think that is?

6. Reread Matthew 26:36–46. What can we learn from Jesus in the garden of Gethsemane about accepting God's will?

Further Study

Long before Steven Covey and other leadership gurus were writing books, Nehemiah completed an ancient version of a SWOT analysis. Nehemiah made a major decision to leave his prestigious role as cupbearer to King Artaxerxes in order to rebuild the walls of his hometown Jerusalem. His thoughtful approach to complex decisions can still instruct us today. Read the first two chapters of Nehemiah. How did Nehemiah approach the decision placed before him? What actions did he take? What can you learn from his decision-making process? Read Nehemiah 4:1–23. How did Nehemiah assess and address threats he encountered when he decided to lead the rebuilding project?

Chapter 7: You've Decided, So Now What?

1. Consider a major decision you made in the past. After the initial wave of relief, did you experience doubt, regret, fear, or fear of missing out? If so, which were most acute for you? How did you combat them?

2. Read Luke 15:11–32. What do we learn about the Father and his response to poor decisions from this parable? Describe a time when you experienced a similarly gracious response after making a poor decision.

3. Think of a time when you made a wise decision. What was your response to this decision? Did it lead you to self-congratulation or to praise of God?

4. What rhythms in your life enable you to remember and rehearse God's past goodness? How might you practically create more time for such rest and remembrance?

5. Read 2 Corinthians 10:5–6. What does Paul instruct us to do with our thoughts? What intrusive thoughts do you need to fight to take captive to the obedience of Christ? What helps you to this end? What hinders you?

6. What next right thing is God calling you to do?

Further Study

Choose one or two of the following psalms as a pattern of praise: 45; 117; 118; 138. Read and meditate upon the psalm(s). How does the psalmist remember and rehearse God's past faithfulness? How does this record of past faithfulness propel the writer into the future? Make your own list or record of God's past faithfulness in your life and past decisions. Consider writing your own poem or song of praise to God.

Appendix

Visual Summaries

The Dashboard of Decisions

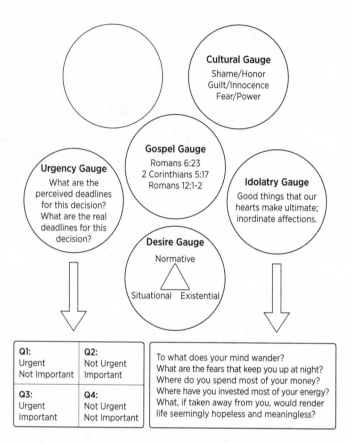

Decision-Making Flowchart

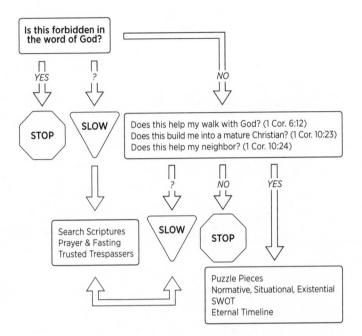

Notes

Introduction

1. Leo Tolstoy, *The Death of Ivan Illyich* (New York: Bantam, 1981), 67.
2. Tolstoy, *Death of Ivan Illyich*, 71.
3. Tolstoy, *Death of Ivan Illyich*, 119–20.
4. C. S. Lewis, *Mere Christianity* (New York: Collier, 1952), 174.
5. Douglas V. Steere, "Foreword," in Thomas Merton, *Contemplative Prayer* (New York: Image, 1996), 10.

Chapter 1: The Drama of Decisions

1. Bruce Waltke, *Knowing the Will of God* (Eugene, OR: Harvest, 1998), 32.
2. For an introduction into Christian hedonism, I would recommend John Piper, *Desiring God: Meditations of a Christian Hedonist* (Portland, OR: Multnomah, 1986); and Jonathan Edwards, *Religious Affections* (Uhrichsville, OH: Barbour, 1999). More recently published, James K. A. Smith, *You Are What You Love: The Spiritual Power of Habit* (Grand Rapids, MI: Brazos, 2016), covers a similar concept and helps to show the role that our affections play in the Christian life.
3. C. S. Lewis, *The Screwtape Letters* (New York: HarperCollins, 2001), 39.
4. A. W. Tozer, *The Pursuit of God* (Camp Hill, PA: Christian Publications, 1982), 73.
5. J. I. Packer, *Evangelism and the Sovereignty of God* (Downers Grove, IL: InterVarsity Press, 2008), 28.
6. Packer, *Evangelism*, 30.
7. Packer, *Evangelism*, 43.

8. Elisabeth Elliot, *Discipline: The Glad Surrender* (Old Tappan, NJ: Power, 1960), 34.

Chapter 2: *The Design of Decisions*

1. Derek Kidner, *Proverbs* (London: Tyndale Press, 1964), 35.
2. Kidner, *Proverbs*, 13–14.
3. Elisabeth Elliot, *A Path through Suffering* (Ann Arbor, MI: Servant, 1990), 184.
4. Sinclair Ferguson, *Grow in Grace* (Carlisle, UK: Banner of Truth, 1989), 28–29.
5. C. S. Lewis, *Mere Christianity* (New York: Collier, 1952), 153.

Chapter 3: *Theological Foundations for Decisions*

1. Bruce Waltke, *Knowing the Will of God* (Eugene, OR: Harvest, 1998), 13.
2. Waltke, *Knowing the Will of God*, 14.
3. G. I. Williamson, *The Westminster Confession of Faith for Study Classes* (Philadelphia: Presbyterian & Reformed, 1964), 46.
4. A. W. Tozer, *We Travel an Appointed Way* (Camp Hill, PA: Christian Publications, 1988), 1.
5. James Petty, *Step by Step: Divine Guidance for Ordinary Christians* (Phillipsburg, NJ: P&R, 1999), 44.
6. George Herbert, *The Country Parson* (New York: Paulist Press, 1981), 251.
7. Jerry Sittser, *The Will of God as a Way of Life* (Grand Rapids, MI: Zondervan, 2000), 29.
8. J. I. Packer, *Knowing God* (Downers Grove, IL: InterVarsity Press, 1973), 92.
9. Packer, *Knowing God*, 93.
10. Sittser, *Will of God*, 34–35.
11. Leslie Newbiggin expounds upon the particular and the universal (focus and scope) as God's pattern of salvation. Lesslie Newbigin, *The Open Secret: An Introduction to the Theology of Mission* (Grand Rapids, MI: Eerdmans, 1995), 68.
12. Petty, *Step by Step*, 120.
13. For a full study of conscience in the Scriptures, I highly recommend *Conscience: What It Is, How to Train It, and Loving Those Who Differ* by Andrew David Naselli and J. D. Crowley (Wheaton, IL: Crossway, 2016).

Chapter 4: *The Dashboard of Decisions*

1. Jayson Georges, *The 3-D Gospel* (Middletown, DE: Time Press, 2017), 11.

2. Georges, *3-D Gospel*, 20.
3. Georges, *3-D Gospel*, 21.
4. Georges, *3-D Gospel*, 25.
5. Georges, *3-D Gospel*, 25.
6. Timothy Keller, *Counterfeit Gods* (New York: Penguin, 2016), *xiv*.
7. Keller, *Counterfeit Gods*, 168.
8. Both Jonah Lehrer and Jonathan Haidt refer to Damasio's studies in their books. While these books are not written from a Christian perspective, they do help to provide evidence that, neurologically, we rely heavily upon emotion and intuition in making decisions. This recent evidence, along with other such studies, helps to debunk the idea that there is such thing as a purely rational decision made by logic alone. Jonathan Haidt, *The Righteous Mind* (New York: Vintage, 2012), 39–41; Jonah Lehrer, *How We Decide* (New York: Mariner, 2009), 13–16.
9. Steven Covey, *The Seven Habits of Highly Effective People* (New York: Fireside, 1990), 151.
10. Charles Hummel, *Tyranny of the Urgent* (Downers Grove, IL: Inter-Varsity Press, 1967).
11. Jerry Sittser, *The Will of God as a Way of Life* (Grand Rapids, MI: Zondervan, 2000), 84.
12. Sittser, *Will of God*, 86.
13. Elisabeth Elliot, *The Music of His Promises* (Ann Arbor, MI: Servant, 2000), 51.
14. Elisabeth Elliot, *Secure in the Everlasting Arms* (Grand Rapids, MI: Revell, 2002), 53.

Chapter 5: Practical Preparation for Decisions

1. Brennan Manning, *Ruthless Trust* (New York: HarperCollins, 2000), 5.
2. Jerry Sittser, *The Will of God as a Way of Life* (Grand Rapids, MI: Zondervan, 2000), 95.
3. Zora Neale Hurston, *Their Eyes Were Watching God* (New York: Harper Perennial, 2006), 21.
4. John Calvin, *Institutes of the Christian Religion*, vol. 1, ed. J. McNeill, trans. F. Battles (Philadelphia, Westminster Press, 1960), 1.1.35.
5. Stuart Briscoe, *Flowing Streams* (Grand Rapids, MI: Zondervan, 2008), 57.
6. Jane Austen, *Persuasion* (New York: Barnes & Noble Classics, 2003), 15.

7. Elisabeth Elliot, *God's Guidance: A Slow and Certain Light* (Grand Rapids, MI: Revell, 1973), 115–16.

8. Elliot, *God's Guidance*, 25.

9. Phillip Keller, *A Shepherd Looks at Psalm 23* (Grand Rapids, MI: Zondervan, 1970).

10. Richard Foster, *Celebration of Discipline* (New York: HarperCollins, 1988), 55.

Chapter 6: Practical Paradigms for Decisions

1. John Frame, *Theology in Three Dimensions* (Phillipsburg, NJ: P&R, 2017), 2.

2. Frame, *Theology in Three Dimensions*, 2.

3. Frame, *Theology in Three Dimensions*, 2.

4. Frame, *Theology in Three Dimensions*, 23.

5. George Ganss, *The Spiritual Exercises of Saint Ignatius: A Translation and Commentary* (Chicago: Loyola Press, 1992), 122.

6. Elisabeth Elliot, *A Path through Suffering* (Ann Arbor, MI: Servant,1990), 69.

Chapter 7: You've Decided, So Now What?

1. Corrie ten Boom, *The Hiding Place* (Bloomington, IN: Chosen, 2001), chap. 2.

2. C. S. Lewis, *The Chronicles of Narnia* (New York: HarperCollins, 2001), 174.

3. Lewis, *Chronicles*, 175.

4. Pamela Roswell, *The Five Silent Years of Corrie ten Boom* (Grand Rapids, MI: Zondervan, 1986), 92.

5. Elisabeth Elliot, *Secure in the Everlasting Arms* (Grand Rapids, MI: Revell, 2002), 71.

6. Elliot, *Secure in the Everlasting Arms*, 130.

Conclusion

1. C. S. Lewis, *The Weight of Glory* (San Francisco: HarperCollins, 1967), 37.

Study Questions

1. Madeleine L'Engle, *Walking on Water: Reflections on Faith and Art* (New York: Convergent, 2016), 17.

2. Frederick Buechner, *Wishful Thinking: A Seeker's ABC* (New York: HarperOne, 1993), 118–19.

General Index

Scripture Index

THE GOSPEL **COALITION**

The Gospel Coalition (TGC) supports the church in making disciples of all nations, by providing gospel-centered resources that are trusted and timely, winsome and wise.

Guided by a Council of more than 40 pastors in the Reformed tradition, TGC seeks to advance gospel-centered ministry for the next generation by producing content (including articles, podcasts, videos, courses, and books) and convening leaders (including conferences, virtual events, training, and regional chapters).

In all of this we want to help Christians around the world better grasp the gospel of Jesus Christ and apply it to all of life in the 21st century. We want to offer biblical truth in an era of great confusion. We want to offer gospel-centered hope for the searching.

Through its women's initiatives, The Gospel Coalition aims to support the growth of women in faithfully studying and sharing the Scriptures; in actively loving and serving the church; and in spreading the gospel of Jesus Christ in all their callings.

Join us by visiting TGC.org so you can be equipped to love God with all your heart, soul, mind, and strength, and to love your neighbor as yourself.

TGC.org

Also Available from
the Gospel Coalition

For more information, visit **crossway.org**.